Terminology

A *lucid dream* is a dream in which the subject is aware that he is dreaming.

A *pre-lucid dream* is one in which the subject considers whether he is dreaming. He may or may not come to the correct conclusion that he is.

An *out-of-the-body* or *ecsomatic* experience is one in which the objects of perception are organized in such a way that the observer seems to himself to be observing them from a point of view which is not coincident with his physical body.

A *Type 2 false awakening* is one in which the subject appears to wake up normally and find himself in bed. His surroundings may at first appear normal, but he gradually becomes aware of something unusual or 'uncanny' in the atmosphere. Alternatively he may 'awake' immediately to a 'stressed' and 'stormy' atmosphere. In either case the subject tends to experience feelings of suspense, excitement or apprehension. He may experience 'hallucinatory' or 'apparitional' effects. If he attempts to move or get out of bed while in this state, he tends to find himself in an ecsomatic state. It is presumed that throughout a Type 2 false awakening the subject is actually lying with his eyes closed, and would appear asleep to an observer.

". . . of great interest to philosophers, to those concerned with the psychology of perception . . . in my opinion, it has implications for the theory of art."—*Professor Colin Cherry*

PSYCHICAL PHENOMENA AND THE PHYSICAL WORLD

Charles McCreery

Research Officer, Institute of Psychophysical Research, Oxford

With a Foreword by
Sir George Joy, K.B.E., C.M.G.

BALLANTINE BOOKS • NEW YORK

© 1973 by the Institute of Psychophysical Research

All rights reserved.

SBN 345-23602-5-125

This edition published by arrangement with Hamish
Hamilton Ltd.

First Printing: November, 1973

Printed in the United States of America

Cover photo by Red Saunders

BALLANTINE BOOKS, INC.
201 East 50th Street, New York, N.Y. 10022

Contents

PART ONE

PART TWO

Acknowledgements

I am grateful to the Society for Psychical Research, Faber and Faber Ltd. and Les Presses Universitaires de France for permission to quote from copyright material. Detailed references will be found at the foot of the pages on which the quotations occur.

Foreword

I welcome this book as an important contribution to the advancement of science.

In the first part of this book Charles McCreery discusses a number of philosophical questions in relation to various psychological and parapsychological phenomena; in these five chapters he has achieved the rare feat of combining intellectual rigour with clarity and readability. Some of the cases given as illustrations are published here for the first time. In my opinion, these first five chapters are a significant contribution to the philosophy of science.

The second part of the book is empirical. In Chapter VI, Mr. McCreery summarizes the results of the Institute of Psychophysical Research's experiments in the field of birth order and extra-sensory perception. The results obtained are of great importance in the search to relate ESP to fundamental personality variables.

The next three chapters constitute valuable

additions to the data already published by the Institute of Psychophysical Research on lucid dreams and out-of-the-body experiences. The Marquis d'Hervey de Saint-Denys's book on dreams was for long relatively inaccessible to researchers. (Freud, for example, in *The Interpretation of Dreams*, refers to it, and remarks that he has been unable to obtain a copy despite all his efforts.) Mr. McCreery has performed a valuable service in making the Marquis's lucid dreams available in an excellent translation.

Chapter VIII deals with an exceptional subject studied by the Institute, and Chapter IX with some salient points from the out-of-the-body experiences reported to the Institute since the publication of its report on this phenomenon.

Finally, in Chapter X, Mr. McCreery describes the experiments carried out in America which have confirmed the prediction made in his earlier book, *Science, Philosophy and ESP*, concerning the acceleration of the alpha-rhythm in the conscious ESP state. This is the first time that a correlation between ESP and a physiological variable has been predicted on theoretical grounds and subsequently confirmed by experiment—a result which, if it continues to be confirmed, will constitute a scientific breakthrough of the first magnitude.

This is a book that can be read with both interest and profit by layman and scientist alike. I wish it the wide readership and the scientific recognition that it deserves.

SIR GEORGE JOY

PART ONE

I

Lucid Dreams

Now I was in a corridor inside the house with my mother and we were setting out on a walk together. I was explaining to her about lucid dreams and she was being tolerant but not really listening. 'Yes, I suppose it's possible,' she said, much as if I'd said, 'The molecule of lysergic acid is related to that of adrenaline,' or 'Perhaps it's a matter of interchanging the time and space axes.' 'We are in a dream *now*, Mother,' I said informatively, as we walked down a winding lane. 'Oh yes,' she said, humouringly. (This situation is rather reminiscent of one I was in with her in waking life when I was about 5, going along a country lane with her and arguing that life might be a dream.) I explained that people might be able to give one another messages in dreams, and she took that all right, but then I said, 'If I tell you something now, will you try to remember it when you wake up?' She jibbed at that. 'Oh, I don't know about *that*,' she said. 'I really don't think I *could*.' 'But you could *try*, couldn't you, Mother?' I said, and with some exhortation she did agree to try (though plainly not very hard). 'Concertina,' I said, loudly and clearly. 'Try to ring me up tomorrow and say that. Concertina, Mother, don't forget.' (This word has just occurred to me as sufficiently unlikely.)[1]

How is one to decide whether one is dreaming or not?

I need scarcely say that pinching oneself is not an adequate criterion. I know of at least two people who have pinched themselves, or got other people to pinch them, in pre-lucid dreams, and in both cases they went on dreaming as before. Each of them concluded after the pinch that he must be awake, but of course he was mistaken. The pinch was just a 'dream pinch', so to speak.

Here is Yves Delage's account of a pre-lucid dream in which he got his daughter-in-law to pinch him to try and determine whether he was awake or not. (A pre-lucid dream is one in which the subject considers whether he is dreaming. He may or may not come to the correct conclusion that he is.)

I find myself dreaming again that, although I should be blind, I am in fact seeing clearly, but I remember that I have had this illusion in dreams before, and that the illusion has been dissipated

_____

[1] Where no reference is given, a case is drawn from the Institute's own files.

on awakening. Then, anxiously, I ask myself: am I dreaming? or am I awake? I feel that this is a difficult problem, and that I am in danger of making a mistake, of drawing a false conclusion, and I try to put together all the considerations which might contribute to a solution. I place myself directly in front of an object which I am looking at; I open my eyes—I see it; I close my eyes—I do not see it (of course, in my sleep, all these movements are completely imaginary). I feel myself, shake myself, stamp my feet to assure myself that I am really awake. On each occasion without exception, I conclude that I am awake. On one occasion in these circumstances, I dreamt that my daughter-in-law was near me. I spoke to her: Louise, I said, look, I am seeing clearly, but I am afraid it is only a dream. Am I really awake? Pinch my arm so that I can be sure of it. She did not answer, but pinched my arm; I could hardly feel the pressure of her hand. 'Harder' I said to her. She obeyed, but no doubt from fear of hurting me, pinched me so gently that I could only just feel it. However, the test seemed to me conclusive; and, to tell the truth, I was so convinced of being awake that I spoke to her less to convince myself than to convince her. Not for a moment did it enter my head to think that if I was dreaming, this verification would prove nothing since it would itself be part of the dream. So I was convinced and very happy.[1]

---

[1] Y. Delage, *Le Rêve*. Les Presses Universitaires de France, Paris, 1919, pp. 450-1; Celia Green's translation.

Here is an example in which one of the Institute's own subjects pinched herself in a lucid dream:

Without any preliminary ordinary dream experience, I suddenly found myself on a fairly large boat travelling at a normal speed up what appeared to be the mouth of a river, just before it issues into the sea. There was some sort of pleasant scenery on either side, with trees and greenery, and straight in front, the water stretched to infinity. The deck was smooth and clean and warmed by the sun, and I felt the warm breeze on my skin. This startled me, because I knew that in a dream one does not feel actual physical sensations with the same intensity and subtlety as in real life, and I was sufficiently mistress of my own thoughts and movements to pinch my arm in order to assure myself that it was only a dream. I felt the flesh under my fingers and the slight pain in my arm, and this filled me with real alarm, because I knew that I ought not to be on that boat, in the daylight. I did not *see* my own body, but I was sufficiently lucid to imagine it, lying inert in my own bed here in Paris . . .

Clearly the subconscious mind is quite equal to the task of inventing a 'hallucinatory' pinch in a dream. Indeed even if we knew of no instance in which it had done so, we could never be sure that one day it would not 'rise to the occasion', and produce something that was indistinguishable from the real thing.

It is important to realize that *all* the senses may be represented in lucid dreams; they are not purely visual. In the following three cases, for example, one subject dreamt of feeling the warmth of the sun; another tasted wine; a third smelled the scent coming from a woman's hair.

I hear their measured tread and watch them from the window of a high house in Galata, in Constantinople, in a narrow lane, one end of which leads to the old wharf and the Golden Horn with its ships and steamers and the minarets of Stamboul behind them. The Roman soldiers march on and on in close ranks along the lane. I hear their heavy measured tread, and see the sun shining on their helmets. Then suddenly I detach myself from the window-sill on which I am lying, and in the same reclining position fly slowly over the lane, over the houses, and then over the Golden Horn in the direction of Stamboul. I smell the sea, feel the wind, and warm sun.[1]

I took the broken glass and threw it out of the window, in order to observe whether I could hear the *tinkling*. I heard the noise all right and I even saw two dogs run away from it quite naturally. I thought what a good imitation this comedy-world was. Then I saw a decanter with claret and tasted it, and noted with perfect clearness of mind: 'Well, we can also have volun-

---

[1] P. D. Ouspensky, *A New Model of the Universe*, Routledge & Kegan Paul, London, 1960, p. 282.

tary impressions of taste in this dream-world; this has quite the taste of wine.'[1]

Seeing a door ajar on the first landing, I entered and found myself in a comfortably furnished bedroom. A young lady, dressed in claret-coloured velvet, was standing with her back to me, tidying her hair before a mirror. I could see that radiant amber sky through the window by the dressing-table, and the girl's rich auburn tresses were gleaming redly in this glamorous light. I noticed that the coverlet of the bed had a crumpled appearance and that there was water in a basin on the washstand. 'Ah, my lady,' thought I, 'you too have been lying down, and now you are making yourself presentable for tea—or is it dinner?'

I did not mind intruding upon her privacy; for she might have no existence outside of my brain, and I knew from previous experiences, that there was small likelihood of my being visible to her. It occurred to me that I would stand just behind her and look over her shoulder into the mirror. I wanted to see whether it would reflect my face. I stood so close to her that I was conscious of a pleasant fragrance emanating from her hair, or perhaps from the soap she had recently used. In the mirror I could see her face—a good-looking one, I think her eyes were grey—but not the faintest indication of mine was visible.[2]

---

[1] F. van Eeden, 'A Study of Dreams', *Proceedings of the Society for Psychical Research*, Vol. XXVI, Part 47, July, 1913, p. 448.

[2] Oliver Fox, *Astral Projection*, University Books Inc., New York, 1962, pp. 77-8.

A subject may also feel an 'imaginary' pain in a dream, i.e. one relevant to his situation in the dream rather than to his 'real' situation of lying in bed. Oliver Fox, for example, once had a lucid dream in which he found himself being tortured, and seemed to experience all the sensations one might expect to have in such a situation in real life, although his body was in fact lying quietly in bed beside his wife. Here is Oliver Fox's account of this experience:

I was naked and bound to an X-shaped framework in a vertical position. Something was trickling down my bare flesh. It was blood from many wounds. I was burning and smarting all over. I could not see, because my sight had been almost destroyed by red-hot irons. Now the colours were moving. They might be the robes of men or women. Every second the pain became more acute, as though an anaesthetic were wearing off. My body seemed to be a mass of wounds and burns and hopelessly mutilated. It was very difficult now not to panic, despite my affirmations that my physical body was in bed at Wimbledon, and I wondered if I might be dying.[1]

As far as we know, any sensation, in any modality, that one can have in waking life, one can have in a lucid or pre-lucid dream. One cannot conclude, therefore, merely from the presence of any particular sensation or sense-da-

---

[1] Oliver Fox, op. cit., pp. 106-7.

tum, however 'realistic' or normal-seeming, and however intense, that one is awake and not asleep.

You may say, 'But when these people tasted wine, smelled scents or felt the warmth of the sun on their skin in lucid dreams there must have been *some* subtle difference between the sensations they experienced and those they would have experienced in similar situations in waking life.' Well, of course there may have been. We can never be sure there wasn't. But if there was, then the subjects themselves were not able to detect it, either at the time or when they woke up. It would therefore have been impossible for them to decide whether they were waking or sleeping merely from examining the quality of their sensations.

꩜

Again, one wants to know, is the lucid dream environment really indistinguishable from the normal environment? The answer seems to be, Yes, at least in certain cases. That is to say, the best lucid dreamers assure one that they are unable, either at the time or subsequently in the waking state, to find any fault with the environment presented to them in a good lucid dream. They may even ask themselves this question at the time, and examine the environment scrupulously for differentiae, without being able to find any. In a pre-lucid dream this may lead them to think that they must be awake, as in the following case.

> Seemed to wake . . . I told X. of the lucid dream I had just been having, and thought of the possibility that this was still a dream. I discussed this with X., but dismissed it because of the naturalness of everything—papers spread out on the carpet under the window, spotted with rain that had come in through it . . . I thought that it could not be a dream, because it could not so accurately reproduce so much in such detail—looking at the numerous papers, feeling their texture, thickness, etc., as I thought this.

Of course, the pre-lucid dreamer in this example might on waking repudiate his judgement that the papers were indistinguishable from real ones. But in fact he does not when questioned on the point. Similarly, in a lucid dream proper, the subject may admire a landscape of tall lacy trees over which he is flying or may observe the texture of glistening wet rocks under electric light, and on waking he may still consider that the scenes were as good as waking life ones.

⌁⊛⌁

Then I was standing at one end of the same room, again aware that I was dreaming. I spoke to a woman I did not know, and she told me she

was a training college lecturer. (I am a teacher)
'Oh no! You're a figment of my imagination,' I
declared, and reached out to grasp her arm. At
this I felt the most tremendous sense of shock,
which was the most vivid moment of the dream.
She was so real, solid, warm and fleshy. I
remember thinking that it was exactly like holding a living arm, and yet I knew I was dreaming
the contact.

We may be inclined to accord some kind of
philosophical primacy to the sense of touch. We
may be tempted to think: 'Of course, I know
one can be mistaken about *visual* appearances
in waking life, and I am prepared to accept that
more or less anything I see at a distance may
not really be there: but *touching* things is different; when I go up to a chair and touch it,
push against it, feeling it resist my passing
through it, then there can no longer be any rea-
sonable doubt: the chair is really there.' Some
such reasoning as this seems to have been implic-
it in Dr. Johnson's mind when he said of Berke-
ley's theory, 'I refute it *thus*', and kicked a
stone. But someone who kicked a stone in a lucid dream might get exactly the same sensations
as Dr. Johnson. In fact, someone might repeat
Dr. Johnson's experiment in a *pre-lucid* dream
in order to determine whether he was awake or
asleep; and if he felt a normal sort of pain and
resistance, he might very well conclude—errone-

ously—that he *must* be awake. Such experiments are in fact not uncommon in pre-lucid dreams. As we have seen, people have tried pinching themselves in pre-lucid dreams, and on feeling a normal pain sensation they have concluded erroneously that they were awake. Furthermore in a lucid dream the objects in one's environment feel just as solid to the touch as the objects in one's environment in waking life. They have a characteristic texture and a characteristic way of resisting the passage of one's hand or foot. The ground on which one walks in a lucid dream may feel just as solid as the ground on which one walks in waking life, and it would no more think of letting one sink into it as if it was not properly solid than would the earth of the waking world.

Descartes suggested as a criterion for distinguishing dreams and waking life that 'dreams are never connected by memory with all the other events of my life, like the things that happen when I am awake'.[1] This is not true of lucid dreams. In a lucid dream a subject remembers his past life in essentially the same way as

[1] Descartes, *Philosophical Writings*, translated and edited by E. Anscombe and P. T. Geach, Nelson, London, 1954, p. 124.

he does when he is awake. He remembers who he is, and what he wants to do now he is lucid, i.e. he remembers any plans or intentions he may have formulated in advance, when he was awake, for what to do when he next had a lucid dream; for example, he remembers that he wants to attempt ESP, or flying, or whatever it may be. He remembers what other people have done in lucid dreams, and what they have written about them in books he has read while awake, and he compares his own experiences with theirs. The following is a typical example.

After a series of somewhat traumatic dreams of escape, I came to what was a sort of drive or brake, at the end of which was a suggestion of a country house behind some trees.

The initiating thought or thoughts were as follows: 'This (i.e., this type of dream) has been going on for ages; it's about time I had a respite!' (This and the next thought were definitely humorous, as it were, though wry or ironic.) Then I thought: Perhaps this qualifies as one of Ouspensky's 'dreams of ways'.

Then the following thoughts definitely took place during the period of lucidity: Shouldn't this be liberating, and more vivid than ordinary dreams? . . .

Also, while still in the dream, I was surprised (and delighted) at having at last achieved a lucid dream. I remembered how it had seemed so difficult in the waking state.

Another experiment I tried was the following:

I thought of Ouspensky's criterion of repeating one's own name. I achieved a sort of gap-in-consciousness of two words: but it seemed to have some effect; made me 'giddy', perhaps; at any rate I stopped. (Perhaps at that point I was already losing the lucidity.)

On waking from a dream such as this the lucid dreamer does not think, 'What a fool I have been; all that was nonsense; I was in an awful muddle in that dream, and remembered everything all wrong', as one may on waking from an ordinary dream. He is more likely to be amazed at the abstruse things he remembered in his lucid dream, such as the result Ouspensky obtained when he repeated his own name in a lucid dream, and he may marvel about how clearly he remembers this, just as clearly, it seems to him, as if he had been thinking about it in waking life.

He may find it difficult to remember specific and immediate details about his daily life, such as his plans for the morrow; but even this type of memory may be subject to a learning effect in lucid dreams. In other words, the more lucid dreams a subject has the easier he may find it to remember the things he wants to in a lucid dream.

We know of no reason why a subject should not remember every detail of his past life in a lucid dream, including the moment of his going to sleep. If he had ordinary dreams on first falling asleep and before becoming lucid, he may remember these in his lucid dream too. Alternatively he may enter a lucid dream state immediately on falling asleep, as Ouspensky was in the habit of doing. In either case the lucid dream is completely continuous with his waking life. The subject can, as Descartes requires, 'connect the perception' of the events in the lucid dream 'uninterruptedly with the whole of the rest of his life'.

⋯⊛⋯

Perhaps the resistance sometimes experienced in lucid dreams to thinking about things that are too 'close up', in time or space, to one's present situation might give one a criterion for deciding whether one was awake or asleep?

Subject E,[1] for example, when she is unable to discover any discrepancy or inconsistency in her dream environment, sometimes tries remembering preceding events to determine whether she is awake or asleep. She writes that once, for example, 'seeming to find myself at the office I tried tracing back the journey from home—the discovery that I was unable to do so led to the realisation that I was dreaming'.

But the trouble is that one may not realize at

---

[1] Cf. Chapter VIII.

the time that there is any difficulty in remembering this kind of thing; one's subconscious may present one with fictitious memories in the dream. For example, one lucid dreamer decided to use as a criterion of a false awakening the question of whether he could remember his plans for the coming day: if he experienced any difficulty in formulating these, this would be a sign that he was not really awake but only in a false awakening. But when he next had a false awakening and applied this test he seemed to be able to remember his plans for the day perfectly well. It was only on awakening properly that he realized that these plans did not correspond with the ones he had actually made, though the dream-plans were perfectly plausible and consistent with his life-style at the time.

❦

You may object that in waking life you are able to check your memories against independent or objective records, such as books, the accounts of other eye-witnesses, and so on. But someone could perfectly well dream that they were checking their memory against an independent source in a pre-lucid dream. People read books in lucid dreams; and they can carry on long conversations with other people. In fact the lucid and pre-lucid dreamer seems to delight in carrying on long discussions with other people in his dreams about the philosophical implications of his situation. For example, if he believes he is dreaming he may argue lucidly that it is safe for him to jump out of the window, while an eye-witness implores him not to just in case it might not be a dream.

I now found myself with X. in a room at the other end of the corridor. I was telling him about the lucid dreams I had just had, and said suddenly as it occurred to me, 'And of course, *this* is a dream now.' X. said with an unhelpful smile, 'Well, it *might* be. How do you know?' 'Of course it is,' I said, and crossed to the window. This was heavily barred; outside were castle-turrets and a long drop below to village roofs. 'I'm going to fly,' I said, and started to break off the bars. They broke as if made of a cross between chocolate and sealing-wax, and I threw the pieces down on to the roofs below. 'Be awkward if it isn't a dream, won't it?' said X., who continued to stand by passively, looking humorous. 'It *is* a dream,' I said firmly, though at the back of my mind I thought cautiously, 'At the worst it couldn't be more than £50 for tiles.'

A dreamer who had considered whether he was dreaming and had decided mistakenly that he was not, could well consult the British Museum on a point of history without realizing that the verification he received would be entirely unreliable. But, of course, if you are asleep any books, people, etc., will be merely dream-books, and dream-people, mere figments of your imagination, and what they tell you will be no more reliable than what you tell yourself.

＊-◎-＊

You might be tempted to say, 'But I know I am awake because I can remember waking up this morning.' But how do you know that your experience of waking up was not a dream also? There is nothing self-contradictory about this idea. It is logically possible to dream about anything at all, including waking up. As a matter of fact some people dream of waking up quite often. They seem to wake, find themselves in bed, and may even get up and start dressing, only to realize at some point that it is all a dream and they have in fact not got out of bed at all.

Yesterday morning I was dreaming and knew I was dreaming because I could walk on the wall, and the door frame was crooked. Anyway, after dreaming awhile I remembered reading in your book that if one says their own name in a dream, that they will wake up. Consequently I said my first name three times and slowly started to wake up. I was a little dizzy because I stood up too fast, and had trouble walking because my 'foot was asleep' (common expression for pressure on nerves from lying on arms or legs wrong). I knew I was no longer dreaming because I could no longer walk on the wall and the door frame was straight. I went to the front door and found a note saying that the police would return some stolen goods that afternoon. (There had been prowlers in the neighbourhood the past week.) The note was very sloppy and had poor grammar. I went into the bedroom and found the stolen items were still there, and much to my surprise, I awoke. It took another minute to straighten things out in my mind.

How do you know that all the experiences you seem to remember having since waking up this morning have not all been part of a dream? You may find this impossible to believe, but can you prove to yourself it is not true?

You may say, 'But I can remember *so much* that has happened since I woke up—in fact it seems ages since I did wake up—surely it would take ages to dream of all that, and one's dreams just don't go on that long.' But one can doze off to sleep in the morning after one's alarm has gone off and seem to have lengthy and complicated adventures in one's dreams, only to find when one does wake up again that only a few minutes have passed. How do you know that the same thing is not happening to you now?

Besides, even if your impression is correct, and it really is a long time since you seemed to wake up, you might just be having a particularly long false awakening. For all we know, a false awakening might last for an indefinitely long time.

You might think, 'But once a person has *rec-ognised* that he is in a false awakening he knows that the *next* time he wakes up he will be well and truly awake.' But unfortunately this is not true. A person may have repeated false awakenings. Each time he seems to wake up and find himself in bed, and each time he realizes sooner or later that he is mistaken and that he is still asleep.

... I ... dreamed that I got out of bed and dressed, and then awoke to find that I was still in bed. Aware of having dreamed about getting up, I got out of bed and dressed. Then again I awoke to find myself *still* in bed. This had me rather startled. I wondered how shall I know when I am *really* awake?

Delage describes one dream in which he 'awoke' four times in succession; only on the fifth occasion did he really wake up and find all four 'wakenings' had been a dream:

This happened when I was in the Roscoff lab-oratory. One night, I was woken by urgent knocking at the door of my room. I got up and asked: 'Who is there?' 'Monsieur,' came the an-swer in the voice of Marty (the laboratory care-taker), 'it is Madame H——' (someone who was really living in the town at that time and was among my acquaintances), 'who is asking for you to come immediately to her house to see Mademoiselle P——' (someone who was really part of Madame H's household and who was also known to me), 'who has suddenly fallen ill.'

'Just give me time to dress,' I said, 'and I will run.' I dressed hurriedly, but before going out I went into my dressing-room to wipe my face with a damp sponge. The sensation of cold water woke me and I realized that I had dreamt all the foregoing events and that no one had come to ask for me. So I went back and to sleep. But a little later, the same knocking came again at my door. 'What, Monsieur, aren't you coming then?'

'Good heavens! So it is really true, I thought I had dreamt it.'

'Not at all. Hurry up. They are all waiting for you.'

'All right, I will run.' Again I dressed myself, again in my dressing-room I wiped my face with cold water, and again the sensation of the cold water woke me and made me understand that I had been deceived by a repetition of my dream. I went back to bed and went to sleep again.

The same scene re-enacted itself almost identically twice more. In the morning, when I really awoke, I could see from the full water jug, the empty bowl, and the dry sponge, that all this had been really a dream; not only the knockings at my door and the conversations with the caretaker, but having dressed, having been in my dressing-room, having washed my face, having believed that I woke up after the dream and having gone back to bed. This whole series of actions, reasonings and thoughts had been nothing but a dream repeated four times in succession with no break in my sleep and without my having stirred from my bed.[1]

Bertrand Russell claims that he experienced 'about a hundred' successive false awakenings on coming round from an anaesthetic.[2] Now there is no reason in principle why someone should not go on experiencing false awakenings for ever without ever waking up. Thus however many times one may seem to have woken up, this does not provide one with any certainty that this time it is the real thing; it always *may* be just another false awakening.

⁓⊛⁓

Nevertheless, although we have not been able to discover any rigorous criterion for deciding whether we are awake or asleep, we none of us are actually in any doubt that we are awake when we are awake. Even if we have fully realized and appreciated the philosophical uncertainty about whether we are awake or not, we actually find it impossible to doubt at any given moment of the day that this is day and not night, so to speak. Why is this? Why do we remain convinced that we are awake when we

---

[1] Y. Delage, *Le Rêve*, Les Presses Universitaires de France, Paris, 1919, pp. 384–5; Celia Green's translation.
[2] Bertrand Russell, *Human Knowledge: Its Scope and Limits*, Allen and Unwin, London, 1948, p. 186.

can apparently find no rational support for this conviction? It is surely because the certainty that one is awake is based, not on any rational computation at all, but on *the way one feels*. One does not say to oneself, 'I have not seen a man walk through a wall for a long time,' or 'I can connect up the events of my past in my memory, therefore I must be awake.' One merely feels, if asked to doubt that one is awake, that of course this is how it *feels* to be awake. Strictly speaking, perhaps, one's conviction is based on memory as well; presumably one is implicitly saying, 'I can remember that I have never had this feeling in dreams, even lucid ones, and I remember that I have always had this feeling in waking life.' But one is not *aware* of making any such computation when one convinces oneself that one is awake. The experience is immediate.

There is an interesting parallel to this in lucid dreams. In a lucid dream the subject is in no doubt at all that it is a dream, and cannot bring himself to doubt this, just as one cannot bring oneself to doubt that one is awake when one is. *Before* becoming lucid the subject may attempt to use rational criteria to decide whether he is dreaming or not—for example, he may try and remember his plans for the morrow; but once he has realized it is a dream, he no longer feels the need to apply any rational criteria to maintain his conviction. It just *feels* like a dream; or the world he is in just has a dream-like texture.

Now this dream-like feeling or texture is quite different from the feeling or texture of waking life.

> I wondered how shall I know when I am *really* awake? It has often puzzled me; but somehow I feel certain that there is a different feeling when one is really awake. I have not yet been able to definitely pin-point the difference. Somehow there seems to be one of the senses missing when one is dreaming—possibly a sense of 'responsibility'.

Subjects may find it difficult to define in words what the difference is, but it is self-evident to them that there is a difference. When I say 'it is self-evident', I mean that they say there is an obvious difference when you talk to them in waking life.

We now seem to have a criterion for deciding whether we are awake or asleep; namely, if you find yourself considering the question at all you can be sure you are asleep! This is because it is only ever in dreams or false awakenings that we consider the matter and remain in any doubt; in waking life, we scarcely ever pause to consider the question, and if we do we are not able to entertain the slightest doubt about it.

Sometimes after a Type 2 false awakening, particularly if the subject is experiencing this phenomenon for the first time, the subject may be in some doubt about whether he was awake or asleep during the experience. An example of this is provided by the experiences of Subject E quoted on pp. 118-119. However, even in this case, although the subject is experiencing doubt while she is awake, what she is in doubt about is whether she was awake or asleep at some time in the past, not whether she is awake or asleep *now*, i.e. at the time of doing the doubting.

This actually might be quite a useful criterion, because in pre-lucid dreams and false awakenings the subject may spend a long time considering whether he is awake or not, and he may come to the wrong conclusion at the end of it. He may decide, for example, that his experience is so like waking life that he *must* be awake. This is quite wrong. Perhaps what the subject should do is to give up trying to decide on rational criteria, and instead try and remember that if he is considering the question at all then he *must* be asleep. There is actually no reason why someone shouldn't be able to remember this in a lucid or pre-lucid dream, because general psychological principles are usually found comparatively easy to recall in these states.

Of course, this is a purely empirical c⟩ rion. It is *possible* that someone might feel e actly like he does when awake even though he was having a lucid dream. Then again, it is *possible* that someone might find himself entertaining prolonged doubts whether he was awake, when he actually was. All someone can say is that neither of these things has ever happened to him yet.

⌐⊙⌐

Hervey de Saint-Denys had an interesting empirical criterion for deciding whether he was awake or asleep. He simply closed his eyes, believing that, if he was asleep, he would soon start to get fresh visual images despite the supposed interposition of his eyelids. It was of the nature of the dream-state to consist of a series of visual images, he thought, and one's subconscious could never resist for long its natural tendency to present one with fresh visual experiences. He writes: 'When one is having certain particularly realistic kinds of dream, one of the best methods for determining whether one is awake or asleep is to cover one's eyes. If one was awake, this would obviously result in permanent darkness. But when one is dreaming, fresh images appear almost at once. The flow of visual imagery is the peculiar characteristic of sleep, and one cannot dream of having one's eyes shut for more than an instant.'[1]

But of course this criterion is at most only an empirical criterion. It was always possible that one day the Marquis might have closed his eyes in a pre-lucid dream, and his subconscious have acted out of character and not obliged him by producing any further visual images until he had dreamt of opening his eyes again.

---

[1] Marquis d'Hervey de Saint-Denys, *Les Rêves et les Moyens de les Diriger*, Cercle du Livre Précieux, Paris, 1964, p. 366.

II

Out-of-the-Body Experiences

... It was summer time, the day bright and sunny and I wore a dress and blazer. I was walking along Brentwood High Street in Essex and there were people shopping and walking near me. As far as I can remember I was thinking of nothing in particular when suddenly I was about 15 ft. above myself and I watched myself walking towards a cinema called the Palace which was a short distance ahead of me, I noticed the people walking round me. I supposed I watched myself walk about 30 to 40 steps and then I was back 'inside' myself again. I felt in no way different and just went on walking along the High St. The whole incident must only have taken a few seconds ...

Are the perceptual experiences of someone undergoing an out-of-the-body experience hallucinatory?

Suppose we define a hallucinatory perception as a perception which the subject experiences without any appropriate or 'justificatory' pattern of stimuli falling on the sensory end-organ concerned. For example, a hallucinatory visual perception of a cat would be one in which the subject saw a cat without any 'cat-shaped' patterns of light quanta falling on his retina. Now clearly a cat—and everything else—seen in an out-of-the-body experience *is* a hallucinatory perception in this sense. The subject's eyes may be completely shut so that no stimuli of any kind can fall on his retina. Even if his eyes are open, he is not having the sort of cat-perception experience that would normally be associated with the pattern of stimuli that are falling on his retina: he may be seeing the cat from above, for example, whereas his eyes are on a level with the cat and are therefore receiving cat-on-a-level-with-the-eye types of stimulus.

But when we say that something is hallucinatory we also mean that we think it is 'not really there' in the outside world. We believe for example that when I have a hallucinatory perception of a cat sitting on the sofa there is not really a cat sitting on the sofa. Now the typical out-of-the-body experience is not hallucinatory in this sense at all. The world the out-of-the-body subject sees before him corresponds to the world seen by other people who are not 'out of the body', in just the same sense as does the world I see before me now. It is the same world; the out-of-the-body subject sees the same room with all its contents, or the same outdoor landscape, as do the people with him, if any. In fact, he sees just what a normal person would do if he were occupying the same position. If the out-of-the-body subject seems to be floating in the air above his house, for example, then he sees just what a normal person would if he were hovering in a helicopter at that point. The following is a case of this type:

A friend & I had travelled from Bedford to St. Albans in order to visit Verulamium. The day was warm, but not hot, one needed a jacket, & there was a slight breeze. When we got to an open, grassy place near to the amphitheatre we sat & ate some sandwiches & fresh apricots to quench our thirst. There were a few people about, but it was not crowded. After sitting & talking for a while we wandered on, talking. Suddenly I seemed to be 50-100 ft. above my body. I could see us both walking along in the shallow bowl of hills, & could see small gestures. I seemed to be floating along above myself rather like a balloon on a string, but I could not see how I was attached, rather I was conscious of moving along to keep pace with my body. My actual body had no sensation whatever & seemed as remote as that of my friend. Reality was my 'floating self' & the objects below seemed as shadows against the reality of my floating self. I could see, but not hear what was going on. It was not frightening, it was peaceful, secure & right. Perhaps I was more conscious than I normally am, probably because it was a new experience. I think I wondered at it at the time. Suddenly I was back in myself. Going out & coming back was like the flick of a switch. During the whole period of time I had continued to walk. Whether I had carried on a conversation or not I could not say, nor do I know how long I was out. Possibly it was only momentary.

Are we justified in calling what the subject does in the out-of-the-body state 'seeing' or should we really call it something else?

If you define seeing as something that you do with your eyes, then clearly the out-of-the-body subject is not *seeing* the world around him. And we can of course arbitrarily decide to call seeing with one's eyes 'seeing' and anything else 'not really seeing'; but this decision is purely verbal and does not advance our knowledge or understanding of the situation.

We might say that seeing with eyes is much more common than the sort of seeing without eyes that goes on in out-of-the-body experiences, therefore what is done with eyes we will call true seeing. But we know of no reason why seeing with eyes should be more common than seeing without; we have no theory of why out-of-the-body experiences should be as rare as they are, and why they should not become the rule rather than the exception.

I was ... in a glass cubicle like 6 others in the ward.

As my temperature was getting higher and higher I became aware that I was no longer in my body but up in the corner of my cubicle watching the nurses flitting about ... bathing the body lying in my bed, etc. I could see through the glass partitions on both sides and could see what the nurses were doing to my neighbours. ... I could hear quite plainly what they said when they were in my cubicle and what the Doctors and Matron said when they came round. . . . I felt no pain, but I sometimes wanted to tell one of the nurses something but could never make her hear. This lasted about 8 or 9 days after which it tailed off as my temperature started to go down then disappeared entirely when I discovered that I was again in my bed and could speak to the nurses.

Let us be quite clear about this: is there anything normal about normal experience except the fact that it is what most of us appear to have most of the time? If we were to discover a race of people who habitually had out-of-the-body experiences most of their waking life, they would doubtless regard any experience in which their point of view did not coincide with that of their physical body as 'normal' and any experience in which their point of view happened to coincide with that of their physical body 'abnormal', or at best a mere variant on normal experience. If social conformity was strong in their society they might even have psychiatrists for ironing out such experiences. 'Doctor, I need help; I don't seem able to see anything except from a point somewhere near my eyes. It's most peculiar; it's never happened to me before. Do you think it could be overwork?'

We might regard their experiences as abnormal. But then so might they regard our pre-occupation with one point of view as abnormal. 'It's all a matter of what you are used to,' one might say. And who is to say which of us is 'right', if indeed either of us are? If both these forms of perception provide the subject with accurate information about the environment, why should we 'prefer' one of them to the other?

Normal experience may seem to have some sort of primacy just because it is normal—i.e. because most of us seem to see things from the point of view of our physical bodies most of the time. But can we give any reason why it should be so, or any reason why it should not be entirely different tomorrow? Can we give any reason why we should not all be having out-of-the-body experiences most of the time? Suppose everybody woke up tomorrow morning to find their 'points of view' irremediably located about six inches above their heads. It is only because such a thing has never yet happened as far as we know that it strikes us as extremely unlikely. We cannot even be certain that there are not people walking about among us now whose points of view are permanently located in this position. Several subjects who had out-of-the-body experiences as children say they gave up trying to tell anyone about them because of the looks they received when they did. Suppose someone was born with his point of view permanently outside his physical body. He might find it impossible or inexpedient to convey the fact to anyone else, and he might go through life without anyone ever being any the wiser. Such an idea may seem fantastic, but we cannot prove it is impossible. As far as we know, such a person could function quite normally; and if he chose to conceal his peculiarity we might never discover it.

─◦◉◦─

Perhaps there is a subjective difference between seeing the external world in the normal state and seeing it in the out-of-the-body state? Subjects tell us that there may be no difference from the subjective point of view: the world may look exactly the same in the out-of-the-body state as it does in the normal state—so much so that the subject may not at first realize that he is not looking at a scene with his physical eyes.

As a pillion passenger on a motor-bike I was involved in a collision with a car. I came off the back of the bike, went over my driver and over the car. I saw the faces of bystanders raised toward me. Then I hit the ground, head first.

I got up from the ground where I lay, surprised that I felt no pain or bruising, and moved away. I saw people running and looked around to see why.

Then I saw that my body was still laying in the road and they were running toward that, some of them passed me as I stood there. I could hear shouts and a woman's voice crying 'She's dead.'

And then a feeling (I can still feel the awful shock of this whenever I recall the incident) of terrible fear came to me. I knew I HAD to return to my body before it was touched. There was a dreadful sense of urgency, or it would be too late. It is this sensation of dread that remains so indelible.

I went back and lay down on top of myself. And as I did so I felt the hardness of the road beneath me and all the terrible pains of bruising, lacerations and concussion that I was subsequently found to be suffering from. . . .

I was moving about thinking I was my normal body. . . . Everything looked normal . . . my 'floating self' behaved exactly as my physical. . . .

The perceptual experiences of the out-of-the-body subject may be as much a source of information to him as the perceptual experiences of someone in the normal state. The out-of-the-body subject is capable of being surprised by what he sees; he uses the information gained by his perceptions to navigate around his environment, and so on. Now we may say, 'Of course, he knows this information all along really; he needn't really be surprised by anything he sees. If he has discovered anything he did not know before he entered the out-of-the-body state, then he has discovered it by ESP. The visual and other experiences are just his subconscious's way of presenting the information obtained by ESP. Of course one *can* be surprised by the products of one's subconscious; we are sometimes surprised and frightened by our dreams, for example. But this does not mean that the out-of-the-body subject's visual and other experiences are really the source of his information.'

The trouble is that this argument can be applied equally well to normal perception. Someone might argue: 'I know that people sometimes experience surprise at the information contained in their visual and other perceptual experiences. And they regard these experiences as the *source* of their information. But this is mere philosophical naiveté on their part. The perceptual experiences are merely their subconscious's way of presenting the information obtained by the senses—the retina, optic tract and so forth. But the subconscious might choose to present the information obtained by the senses in a quite different form, in hunches, intuitions, or a small internal voice, for example.'

⁓⊛⁓

You may feel tempted to say: 'I know that what the out-of-the-body subject sees in his experience is veridical; but he is still not *seeing the external world* in the same sense as he does in the normal state. He is merely having hallucinatory perceptions which happen to correspond to what is actually there in the outside world. In an out-of-the-body experience the subject is obtaining information about his environment by means of ESP and he is merely rationalizing it in the form of visual and other modes of hallucinatory perception. These hallucinatory perceptions are merely a convenient form in which his subconscious may present to consciousness the information it already possesses.'

This is a perfectly valid interpretation of what goes on in an out-of-the-body experience, and no-one could at present disprove it. But the trouble is that it is an equally valid interpretation of what goes on in the normal state. Someone may perfectly well argue, 'I don't believe that eyes have anything to do with seeing. I believe that even in the normal state we gain all our information about our environment by means of ESP, and we merely rationalize it in the form of visual and other hallucinations. The so-called 'optical apparatus', with its nervous impulses and so on, is either just a blind—perhaps to re-assure people that there is no such thing as action at a distance—or else serves some quite other function as yet unknown.' Now this may seem rather an eccentric theory; but this does not mean that it is a logically impossible one. Its proponent might even say, 'My theory has the advantage that it only posits the existence of one process to explain what is going on in both the normal state and out-of-the-body experiences. I admit that the exact nature of ESP is not yet known, but neither is the process by which someone "makes use of" the information supplied by his optic nerve, and "transforms" it into visual experiences.'

It is difficult to see how we can distinguish between *seeing the world* and *having hallucinatory perceptions which happen to correspond to the world*. If someone cares to describe normal perception as 'having hallucinatory perceptions which happen to correspond to the real world' how are we to stop him? We do not normally talk in such terms because it is a rather longwinded way of describing things. But this does not mean that it is philosophically inadmissible. Let us try and imagine two people, one of whom is really perceiving the world and the other merely having hallucinatory perceptions which happen to correspond to the world around him. It is difficult to see how we could detect any difference between them. What test could we employ? Of course, there may be some difference, but if there is we do not know what it is.

Again, imagine that due to a genetic mutation someone was born into the world who did not perceive the world normally as we do, but who happened to have hallucinatory experiences that corresponded to the world. So long as his experiences always corresponded to the world and there was never any inconsistency between his hallucinatory experiences and the 'genuine' perceptual ones that we were having or would have had in his place, then we would never be able to detect anything peculiar about him—we should never be able to catch him out, so to speak. Now how do you know that you are not such a person? As long as your hallucinatory experiences never let you down and never fail to correspond to the real world, you will never discover that you are any different from other people. For that matter, might we not all be hallucinating instead of having 'proper perceptions'? So long as we all have mutually consistent hallucinatory perceptions, and they all correspond to the real world, we will never discover that what we are having is not the real thing. How then can we say that the subject of the out-of-the-body experience is having hallucinatory perceptions but we are not?

~◈~

Imagine a world of disembodied beings. They can locomote by will-power, like the subject of an out-of-the-body experience, and they interact with their environment by psychokinesis. But although they can communicate with each other by telepathy, the one thing they find difficult is letting each other know where they are. They have to go through a laborious rigmarole like this: 'I am six feet above the dark-looking rock at the end of the row of pine trees, etc.' So, as a kind of short-hand, to save themselves the trouble of perpetually relating their point of view to objects in their communal environment, they decide that each of them will think up for himself a hallucinatory 'body' which will be visible to the others. Just how can they make their 'bodies' visible to each other? Well, each of them can make use of telepathy, and therefore knows the intentions of the other; so each knows where the other is having the hallucinatory experience of 'occupying a body' and agrees that he himself will hallucinate a body having exactly the same characteristics in just the spot the first person is intending to 'occupy'. This may seem as roundabout a way of communicating one's position as simply using telepathy, but it is a perfectly possible set-up, even if we may happen to think it an unlikely one.

But now let us suppose that our mythical beings are still not satisfied. They have labelled the position of each being with a particular kind of seemingly physical object which they call a body, but they still find it difficult to predict where any particular body is to be found at a given time. This is because our beings locomote by will-power, you will remember, and so far they have only agreed to hallucinate a body where they know by telepathy the other person to be viewing the world. This agreement obviously does not put any limitation on the speed with which any particular body moves about their communal environment. If person A decides to 'travel' a hundred miles in a second or two and have a look at some friends there, then everyone else just has to hallucinate his 'body' in the new location, or, in the case of those who are in the location he has just left, not hallucinate him at all.

Now perhaps a certain jealousy of each other's freedom of movement gets into these mythical beings. At any rate, they agree to hallucinate 'bodies' that actually obey the physical laws of their world, as well as looking just like physical objects. Hereafter, they find they can predict each other's movements much better, because although person A may still take it into his head to go and visit his friends a hundred miles away, he can now only get there at a certain finite speed determined by the laws of gravitation, etc., or their equivalent in our imaginary world.

But still our mythical beings are not satisfied. Although their new 'bodies' now obey the laws of physics, they find that the actions of the people associated with them do not obey laws at all; in other words they are all still using psychokinesis to interact with their environment, and by-passing their bodies so to speak. 'This must stop', they decide. 'We cannot have people going round doing miracles any more, and producing utterly unpredictable effects on the environment. It is not compatible with the dignity of having a body.' So they all agree only to use PK to produce effects compatible with their supposed bodies interacting with the environment, and they invent physiologies for these bodies which operate according to certain specific laws and limit the kinds of operations they can perform on their environment—at least so long as they remember the laws. Having social consciences they do remember them most of the time, so only occasionally does a slip up occur and someone do a miracle.

Now suppose that this race of beings were suddenly smitten with an obscure disease which produced selective amnesia and made them forget that they had made the collective decision to hallucinate a body where they knew a person to be, and to make his body obey the laws of physics, etc. And suppose that nevertheless the force of habit made them go on hallucinating these bodies, and obeying these laws. Then they might well come to think their bodies had just the same status as any other object in their environment, just as we do.

There is no physical test they could apply to distinguish between their bodies and other objects in their environment because, by the prior, forgotten arrangement, each of them will hallucinate just those results to any given test as would be obtained if it was performed on a real, physical object.

You may think that if some outsider from another planet were to visit our mythical people he would see nothing of these imaginary bodies of theirs, and if he were nevertheless to become aware of their existence—by telepathy, let us say—he could readily disabuse them of their belief that they possessed physical bodies. But would they believe him? Would they not call him a madman to doubt the existence of something that every normal person could see? They might say: 'You are merely having a negative hallucination whenever you see a physical body. It is probably something to do with your upbringing.' And how could he ever prove to them that they were wrong?

III

Apparitions

At the time I was either sewing or talking to my baby, I cannot remember quite what I was doing at that moment. The baby was on the bed. I had a very strong feeling I must turn round; on doing so I saw my brother, Eldred W. Bowyer-Bower. Thinking he was alive and had been sent out to India, I was simply delighted to see him, and turned round quickly to put baby in a safe place on the bed, so that I could go on talking to my brother; then turned again and put my hand out to him, when I found he was not there. I thought he is only joking, so I called him and looked everywhere I could think of looking. It was only when I could not find him I became very frightened and had the awful fear that he might be dead.[1]

Let us consider what are the differences between an apparition and a normal figure. What do we have in mind when we implicitly contrast the two?

---

[1] *Proceedings of the Society for Psychical Research*, Vol. XXXIII, p. 170.

I think one's first reaction is to say that a person is 'really there' whereas an apparition is not. But what do we mean by this? It is hard to define one's concept of a person, but I think what we mean is that there is a consciousness behind the appearances we call 'John Smith', for example. We do not think there is any consciousness behind the appearances we call 'the apparition of John Smith'; we think that there is nothing but the appearance.

Needless to say, this is not something that we can 'prove' by direct experience. It is more a metaphysical or theoretical interpretation of our experience, and it may or may not be justified. So what we must do if we are to define the difference between an apparition and a real person is to describe the differences between our *experience* of an apparition and our experience of a real person. We must enumerate their behavioural or observable differences.

Well, first, a normal person 'lasts longer'. That is to say, he does not suddenly disappear, as an apparition may do. Or, if he does, there is some physical reason for his disappearance, such as that he has trodden on a bomb. We think of a normal person as a more or less permanent part of our environment.

But this does not give us an infallible criterion for distinguishing between an apparition and the 'real thing'. For theoretically an apparition might last for ever. At least, we do not at present know of any reason why it should not. It might become just as familiar and predictable a part of our environment as a normal person.

The second difference between an apparition and a normal person is that the normal person interacts with his environment whereas an apparition characteristically leaves no physical trace of his presence. For example, if an apparition goes from one room to another he will appear to walk through the door, or, if the door does appear to open, it will later be found that this was part of the apparition, so to speak, and that the door really remained closed all the time.

The bedroom door was shut all night on this occasion, and I was lying awake when I saw the door open and someone peep round. I thought it was one of our assistants come for a lark to pull me out of bed ... however, I lay still, and then the door seemed to open wide, so I leaned out of bed to give it a hard push and everything vanished, and I nearly fell out of bed, for the door was shut as when I went to bed.[1]

But this again does not provide us with a criterion for classifying a normal person as superior to or more real than an apparition. This

---

[1] *Proceedings of the Society for Psychical Research*, Vol. XXXIII, p. 365.

is because of the possibility of psychokinesis. It is theoretically possible that an apparition might be accompanied by PK effects, so that it appeared to interact with its environment just like an ordinary person. For example, a door might blow open by PK, and at the same time an apparition might go through the motions of turning the door's handle and opening it. This phenomenon, or conjunction of phenomena, would surely be indistinguishable to an observer from a real person opening a door.

Here is a case in which the percipient appears to interact with the apparition as if it was a normal person:

As I said, I was going along P. Street—it might be some six or eight days before the great St. Leger day. I generally had a pound or two on the 'Leger' and it was my intention, as soon as my little order was given for stationery, to see a friend about the horse I had backed. Crossing from left to right in P. Street, whom should I meet (or as I thought met) but an old customer, as he had been for some years, of my father's; my father was formerly a brewer, and he had supplied the party I had met with ale, as I said, for some years, and I used to collect the accounts from him along with others in the same line: he was a beerhouse-keeper, or as they were then called a jerry-shopkeeper. I went up to him, called him by his right name, shook him by the *left hand*, for he had *no right*, it having been cut off, when he was a youth; he had a substitute for a hand in the shape of a hook, and he was, said he, very active with this hook when his services were required in turning anyone out of his house that was in any way refractory; he was what you might call a jolly, good, even-tempered sort of a man, and much respected by his customers, most of whom did a little betting in the racing line. He had a very red countrified sort of a face, and dressed quite in a country style, with felt hat, something after the present style of billy-cocks, with thick blue silk handkerchief and round white dots on it, his coat, a sort of chedle-swinger, and a gold watchguard passing round his neck and over his waistcoat; his clothing was all of good material and respectably made. The moment he saw me his face shone bright, and he seemed much pleased to meet me, and I may say I felt a similar pleasure towards him. Mind, this occurred in perfect daylight, no moonlight or darkness so essential an accompaniment to ghost stories; many people were passing and repassing at the time. You may be sure I did not stand in the middle of the street for about seven minutes talking and shaking hands with myself; someone would have had a laugh at me had that been the case. I almost at once, after the stereotyped compliments of the day, launched into the state of the odds respecting the St. Leger, and into the merits and demerits of various horses. He supplied me with what information I required, and we each went our way. He was a man considered to be well posted up in such matters, had cool judgment and discrimination; in fact, he was one of those that would not be led away by what are called tips. I made a memorandum or two, shook his hand again, and passed on about my business, ordered my catalogues, etc.

I came back sauntering along towards the office, not now intending to see the party I had previously intended to see. As I got to the same part of P. Street, on my way back, I suddenly stood still, my whole body shook, and for the moment I tried to reason with myself. The man I had been speaking to was dead some four years before![1]

The third difference between an apparition and a real figure is that an apparition may not be visible to all those who would be expected to see it if it was a normal figure. In everyday life there is no class of persons who are only visible to certain types of people and are invisible to the rest. But an apparition may be seen by some, all, or only one of a number of people together in a room.

The trouble is we are quite unable to predict who will see an apparition on a given occasion and who will not. The same person may see an apparition on one occasion and on a later occasion fail to see anything when other people present are reporting an apparition's presence. It may even be apparently the same apparition on each occasion, as in the Morton case.

In the following instance both the narrator,

---

[1] Sir Ernest Bennett, *Apparitions & Haunted Houses*, Faber and Faber, 1939, pp. 173-4.

Miss R. C. Morton, and her sister saw the apparition at one point, and then a moment later Miss R. C. Morton saw it but her sister did not. (The 'figure' that the narrators refer to in the two passages below was that of a tall lady, dressed in black, whose face was hidden in a handkerchief held in her right hand.)

On the evening of August 11th we were sitting in the drawing-room, with the gas lit but the shutters not shut, the light outside getting dusk, my brothers and a friend having just given up tennis, finding it too dark; my eldest sister, Mrs. F., and myself both saw the figure on the balcony outside, looking in at the window. She stood there some minutes, then walked to the end and back again, after which she seemed to disappear. She soon after came into the drawing-room, when I saw her, but my sister did not.[1]

In the next extract, which concerns a separate incident, the narrator is Miss R. C. Morton's sister, Edith Morton.

The next time I saw the figure was one evening at about 8 o'clock in July, 1885, a fine evening and quite light. I was sitting alone in the drawing-room singing, when suddenly I felt a cold, icy shiver, and I saw the figure bend over me, as if to turn over the pages of my song. I

---

[1] Miss R. C. Morton, 'Record of a Haunted House', *Proceedings of the Society for Psychical Research*, Vol. 8, 1892, p. 317.

called my sister, who was in another room. She came at once, and said she could see it still in the room, though I then could not.[1]

There is, however, a class of apparitions that are seen by all those in a position to see them. And if this class of apparition also had the characteristics of subsisting indefinitely and being conjoined with PK effects at the points at which they interact with their environment, then it is difficult to see how we should ever be able to detect their existence or distinguish them from normal people.

≈⊛≈

An apparition can be completely life-like. In face it can provide such an exact imitation of a normal figure that the percipient does not realize at the time that it *is* an apparition.

The following is a case of this kind. The percipient was a Miss Ellen Carter, the daughter of a launderess in the employment of a Mrs. Benecke. Miss Carter saw an apparition of Mrs. Benecke's son, Edward, on the day that he was killed in a climbing accident in the Swiss Alps.

On Tuesday, July 16th, 1895, between the hours of 1 and 2 o'clock, I was doing some work in our bedroom and, looking out of the window,

---

[1] Ibid., pp. 324–5.

saw (as I thought) Mr. Edward Benecke with another young gentleman walking in the garden, and I went at once to mother and told her Mr. Edward had come home, and she said something must have prevented him from starting, as we knew he was going to Switzerland for his holiday, for I was positive it was him I saw. When nurse came in on the Thursday, mother asked her if Mr. Edward had come home, and she said 'No' and then we only said 'I thought I saw him,' and we thought no more about it until the sad news reached us. . . .

I did see another young man with Mr. Edward (as I thought it was) and the look was not momentary, for I was so surprised to see him that I watched him until he turned round the path; he was coming, as he sometimes did after luncheon, from the stable yard, along the path and turned towards the house. He was smiling and talking to his friend, and I particularly noticed his hair, which was wavy as it always was; he had nothing on his head. It was all that that made me feel so sure it was him, and I felt that I could not have been mistaken, knowing him so well. I cannot tell you anything [about] what the other young gentleman was like, as he was walking the other side; also I hardly noticed him at all, being so surprised to see Mr. Edward. Mother was doubtful when I told her about it and said I must be mistaken; but I said I was sure I was not, and I was positive I had seen him, and I felt sure he had come home until nurse came in and said he had not been home, and then I thought how strange it was, and even then I could not think I was so mistaken, and often have I thought about it and feel even now that it was him I saw. Mother did say perhaps some accident had happened to his friend that he was to travel with and so was prevented from going; that was the only remark that was made about an accident.[1]

Cases such as this obviously remind one of those out-of-the-body experiences in which the subject does not realize at first that it *is* an out-of-the-body experience and not just a continuation of his normal life. In both the apparitional and the out-of-the-body experience it is the realism of the perceptual experience that 'fools' the subject. Yet in the apparitional experience the percept does not correspond to anything that is really there and in the out-of-the-body experience the percept occurs apparently without the subject using his eyes.

In some apparitional cases the subject does not realize *at first* that he is seeing an apparition, but then realizes it while still seeing the apparition; in other cases the subject does not realize till after the apparition has gone that it was an apparition. Sometimes he realizes this just because it goes, i.e. because it disappears in an abnormal fashion, and sometimes because of information given to him by other people, e.g.

---

[1] *Proceedings of the Society for Psychical Research*, Part LXXXVI, October, 1922, pp. 184-5.

that the person whom he saw is actually on the other side of the country or even dead. Might there not be cases in which the subject *never* realizes that it is an apparition?

Let us imagine that one is looking out of a window onto a crowd of people walking along a pavement. How is one to know that one of them is not an apparition, and not a real person at all? An apparition might certainly be mixed in with all the real people and not be noticed, to judge from descriptions of apparitions that were eventually identified as such.

'But,' you may say, 'I know that in principle I could go up to any one of those people on the street and question them. I know that the mere fact of his answering me coherently would not prove he was not an apparition, because people have occasionally spoken with apparitions; but suppose he gave me his name and address and I was subsequently able to verify that a person of his description lived there. Surely you could not then doubt that he was a real person.' But people have been known to hallucinate houses and physical objects generally, as in the following case.

I came to live at Rougham, four miles from Bury St. Edmunds, in 1926. The district was then entirely new to me, and I and my pupil, a girl of fourteen, spent our afternoon walks exploring it.

One dull, damp afternoon, I think in October '26, we walked off through the fields to look at the church of the neighbouring village, Bradfield St. George. In order to reach the church, which we could see plainly ahead of us to the right, we had to pass through a farm-yard, whence we came out on to a road. We had never previously taken this particular walk, nor did we know anything about the topography of the hamlet of Bradfield St. George. Exactly opposite us on the further side of the road and flanking it, we saw a high wall of greenish-yellow bricks. The road ran past us for a few yards, then curved away from us to the left. We walked along the road, following the brick wall round the bend, where we came upon tall, wrought-iron gates set in the wall. I think the gates were shut, or one side may have been open. The wall continued on from the gates and disappeared round the curve of the road.

Behind the wall and towering above it was a cluster of tall trees. From the gates, a drive led away among these trees to what was evidently a large house. We could just see a corner of the roof above a stucco front in which I remember noticing some windows of Georgian design. The rest of the house was hidden by the branches of the trees.

We stood by the gates for a moment, speculating as to who lived in this large house, and I was rather surprised that I had not already heard of the owner amongst the many people who had called on my mother since our arrival in the district. This house was one of the nearest large residences to our own, and it seemed odd that the occupants had not called. However, we then turned off the road along a foot-path leading away to the right to the church which was perhaps under a hundred yards off. On leaving the church, we cut down through the churchyard into the fields and home, without returning to the road or to the farm-yard. It was then drizzling rain.

On arriving home, we discussed the big house and its possible occupants with my parents, and then thought no more of it.

My pupil and I did not take the same walk again until the following spring. It was, as far as I can remember, a dull afternoon with good visibility in February or March. We walked up through the farm-yard as before, and out on to the road, where, suddenly, we both stopped dead of one accord and gasped. 'Where's the wall?' we queried simultaneously. It was not there. The road was flanked by nothing but a ditch, and beyond the ditch lay a wilderness of tumbled earth, weeds, mounds, all overgrown with the trees which we had seen on our first visit.

We followed the road on round the bend, but there were no gates, no drive, no corner of a house to be seen. We were both very puzzled. At first we thought that our house and wall had been pulled down since our last visit. But closer inspection showed a pond and other small pools amongst the mounds where the house had been visible. It was obvious that they had been there a long time.

Yet, we were both independently certain that we had seen house and wall on our previous visit, and our recollections coincided exactly. I should mention that my pupil was neither imaginative nor suggestible, and that we were sufficiently good friends to permit her to disagree with me firmly had she wished to do so.

We then returned home, half amused, half bothered, and yet convinced that we *had* seen that wall and house on the occasion of our first visit. We mentioned the matter to my parents, who, though not altogether incredulous, thought that we must have been mistaken. They don't think so now. Later, I made various tentative inquiries of some villagers who lived near the site of our mystery, but they had never heard of a house existing at that spot, and obviously thought my question a foolish one, so I let the matter drop.[1]

Furthermore, several people can perceive an apparition collectively. It is theoretically possible that we are all collectively hallucinating a given person, his house and all the signs of his existence. It might be objected that no known collective apparition has gone on as long as this or been so complicated. But this does not prove that one might not suddenly do so. Furthermore, it may be that collective apparitions *have* gone on a long time in the past—so long that we have never detected them.

---

[1] Sir Ernest Bennett, *Apparitions & Haunted Houses*, Faber and Faber, 1939, pp. 363-5.

Of course, you may object that an apparition is not 'solid' like a real person. People are quite often touched by apparitions and the sensation they get may be perfectly normal, i.e. just the same as the sensation they would get if they were touched in that particular way by a normal person. But if the percipient tries to touch the apparition he usually finds that his hand goes through it.

But again, if the apparition was conjoined with an appropriate PK effect resisting the passage of the percipient's hand just when it appeared to reach the surface of the apparition, then presumably the apparition might be indistinguishable from a normal person.

For example, imagine the following phenomena conjoined with an apparitional figure.

On other occasions, Eusapia being securely held hand and foot, outside the cabinet, I have gone into the cabinet during the height of a séance, and taken hold of the small séance-table, upon which the musical instruments were placed. I could see across the table; see that nothing visible was there; yet an invisible 'being' of some sort wrestled with me for the possession of the table, and finally succeeded in throwing myself and the table completely out of the cabinet— though I have always been considered quite athletic, and done much boxing, etc., in my younger days. All this, be it remembered, when nothing visible held the opposite side of the table, and when the medium was held very securely hand and foot, by two sitters, *outside* the cabinet.[1]

You may suggest that a physical object can be photographed whereas an apparition can not. Strictly speaking this is still only a presumption, since as far as I know no one has yet been in a position to photograph an apparition under suitable conditions. Miss Morton, for example, for some time kept a camera at the ready, but whenever she used it to photograph the apparition it was too dark for anything to come out at all.

Of course, the fact that many apparitions, such as that in the Morton case, are seen by some of those present, but not by all, may create a strong presumption in one's mind that such an apparition would not be photographable. But strictly speaking, this is just a fact about human psychology, and it is logically possible that an apparition might be seen by only some of those who looked at it and yet come out on a film exposed in its direction. The photographic plate might in principle be affected by PK, regardless of how many people had the

---

[1] Hereward Carrington, *Modern Psychical Phenomena*, Kegan Paul, Trench, Trubner and Co., London, 1919, p. 103.

visual experience of 'seeing' the apparition. Let us imagine that the appearance of an apparition was always conjoined with a PK effect, such that, whenever a camera was pointed in its direction, the film was so affected that an appropriate 'photograph' was obtained just as if it had been pointed at an ordinary person. Then we would not be able to distinguish this apparition from a real person merely by photographing it and observing the result.

IV

Materializations

On at least one occasion I have held a 'materialized' hand in mine and felt it dissolve within my own grasp. It was *not* pulled away, but slowly disintegrated. The grasp must have lasted four or five seconds, and during that time I carefully noted the structure of the hand. It appeared to be lifelike and fairly warm, slightly larger than Eusapia's, possessing bones, skin, hair, finger-nails, etc., like an ordinary flesh-and-blood hand. Yet the next instant it was gone! I was at the time standing about four feet from the medium, who remained seated at the table, both her hands visibly controlled. It was fairly light at the time, and I could see the arm, visible as far as the elbow—and nothing beyond! It was a most impressive experience.[1]

In fact a class of 'apparition' has been reported that fulfils all the criteria we mentioned in the

---

[1] Hereward Carrington, *The American Séances with Eusapia Palladino*, Garrett Publications, New York, 1954, p. 272.

last chapter except the one about duration. The so-called 'materializations' of Eusapia Palladino were, as far as one can tell, visible to all those in a position to see them. At any rate, I know of no instance in which someone present is reported as failing to see anything when there was no obvious reason why he should not see it. For example, we do not read: 'X and Y reported seeing a clearly defined hand, but Z was unable to verify this observation although the level of illumination was good and he made every attempt to see what X and Y were pointing out to him.' Instead we find it everywhere implicitly assumed that the materializations were like physical objects in this respect and could be seen by everyone, or if they could not be so seen it is usually implied that this was due to the level of illumination prevailing at the time or the interposition of some physical object such as the table. Secondly, the materializations of Eusapia Palladino interacted with their environment like normal physical objects. If a hand was seen to knock a bell off the table, for example, the bell would actually fall to the floor in the normal way and remain there even after the sitting had ended if no-one happened to pick it up. Thirdly, the materializations appear to have been photographable.

But of course, sooner or later the materializations 'dematerialized', so to speak. One might grasp one of the materialized hands, for example, and for a time feel it warm and firm in one's grip just like a normal hand; but eventually it would seem to 'melt away' or dissolve in one's grasp.

༤❀༣

How can we distinguish between apparitions and 'materializations'?

As we have seen, an apparition characteristically does not interact with its environment in the way a normal physical object would, whereas a materialization does. For example, the Morton apparition appeared to walk straight through threads stretched across its path, leaving them undisturbed. Here is Miss Morton's account of her experiments:

I have several times fastened fine strings across the stairs at various heights before going to bed, but after all others have gone up to their rooms. These were fastened in the following way: I made small pellets of marine glue, into which I inserted the ends of the cord, then stuck one pellet lightly against the wall and the other to the banister, the string being thus stretched across the stairs. They were knocked down by a very slight touch, and yet would not be felt by anyone passing up or down the stairs, and by candle-light could not be seen from below. They were put at various heights from the ground, from 6 inches to the height of the banisters, about 3 feet.

I have twice at least seen the figure pass through the cords, leaving them intact.[1]

But now let us suppose that the Morton figure had broken the threads as it walked through them, just as a normal person would. We could now account for this by saying that the figure was a materialization after all. Or we could continue to maintain that it was an apparition, and assert that the breaking of the threads was a PK effect, produced by whoever was responsible for the apparition, and timed to coincide with the apparition's reaching the obstacle, so as to provide an additional touch of verisimilitude.

Again, consider the following case in which all those present at the time see an apparition:

As the weather became more wintry, a married cousin and her husband came on a visit. One night, when we were having supper, an apparition stood at the end of the sideboard. We four sat at the dining-table; and yet, with great inconsistency, I stood as this ghostly visitor again, in a spotted, light muslin summer dress, and without any terrible peculiarities of air or manner. We all four saw it, my husband having attracted our attention to it, saying, 'It is Sarah,' in a tone of recognition, meaning me. It at once disappeared.

---

[1] Miss R. C. Morton, 'Record of a Haunted House', *Proceedings of the Society for Psychical Research*, Vol. VIII, Part XXII, July 1892, p. 321.

None of us felt any fear, it seemed too natural and familiar.

The apparition seemed utterly apart from myself and my feelings, as a picture or statue.[1]

This would normally be regarded as a case of a collective apparition. But if someone cared to assert that it was an isolated case of 'materialization' could we prove him wrong?

Someone might also say that Eusapia's materialized hands were merely collective apparitions, and that the movement of the bell, for example, was merely a PK effect timed to coincide in time and place with the appearance of the hand so as to make it seem that the hand was knocking the bell in the normal way.

～⊙～

How can we distinguish between a 'materialization' and a physical object?

As we have seen, a materialized hand produced by Eusapia Palladino, for example, did not last indefinitely but 'faded away' after a greater or lesser period of time. And as far as I know, no materialization has ever lasted more than a matter of minutes. But the trouble is that we know so little about the nature of materializations that we know no reason why one

---

[1] E. Gurney, F. W. H. Myers & F. Podmore, *Phantasms of the Living*, Vol. II, Trübner and Co., 1886, pp. 217-18.

should not last indefinitely. This may seem unlikely. But supposing it did happen, would we have any means of distinguishing the resulting materialization from a real physical object?

We may ask ourselves whether there is not some other discernible difference, in addition to that of duration, between one of the materializations of Eusapia Palladino and a real object. We naturally tend to feel that there is some essential difference. We feel that the materialization is in some way just a counterfeit or a sham, and that if we could 'get behind it', so to speak,—get behind the appearance—we should be able to expose it, and show that its pretentions to being a physical object were unfounded. But is this feeling justified? What does it amount to in terms of verifiable predictions about the materialization's behaviour?

I think the first thing one thinks of is that the materialized hand, for example, would not have a normal molecular structure like a proper physical object. But does one have any justification for this expectation? Let us imagine that a materialized hand stayed in existence long enough for us to examine its internal structure under a microscope. What would we expect to see? We would hardly expect to see nothing. What after all does 'examining something under a microscope' come to? Someone looking through the eyepiece has a certain characteristic set of visual experiences. Now let us suppose you hold the view that Eusapia's ability to produce 'materializations' consisted of her somehow being able to induce all those present to have a mutually consistent form of collective hallucination. There seems no reason why the subconscious of Eusapia Palladino should not also 'make up' a set of visual experiences for someone looking through a microscope at one of her materialized hands in just the same way as it 'made up' the visual experiences of those present at her séances.

Of course you may choose to think of the materialization phenomenon as Eusapia Palladino 'creating' a physical object to stand on a par with all the other physical objects in the room and existing independently of anyone perceiving it. But again in this case it would be strange if the object had no internal structure at all. There seems no reason why Eusapia should not create electrons and protons and all the other microscopic constituents of a hand, say, if she was able to create its macroscopic structure. If not, where did her powers leave off, so to speak, and why?

Of course in either view of the materialization, it can be argued that Eusapia was too ignorant to be able to 'dream up' an internal structure for a hand. She would never have heard of electrons or protons, let alone know how they ought to be arranged in a hand. But this is rather a contingent difficulty. Someone else who was able to produce materialization phenomena might very well know all about electrons and protons. Also we are not allowing for the possibility of ESP. Eusapia might have found out about the internal structure of objects by ESP and then worked in her knowledge in constructing her materializations. So we cannot rule out the possibility that someone might produce a materialization that passed all the microscopic tests scientists were able to make on it.

V

Psychokinesis

Sometimes when she [Eusapia Palladino] is going to push a distant object she will make a little sudden push with her hand in its direction, and immediately afterwards the object moves. Once this was done for my edification with constantly the same object, viz. a bureau in a corner of the room, but with the group of observers and medium (under control as usual of course) first close to it and then gradually further and further away from it, and I was instructed by the agency to observe that the time-interval between the push and the response increased as the distance increased, so that when 6 or 7 feet away the time interval was something like 2 seconds.[1]

When we think about psychokinesis we get a feeling of inconceivability when we contemplate the gap between the thing moved—a table on the other side of the room, say—and the per-

---

[1] Sir Oliver Lodge, *Journal of the Society for Psychical Research*, Vol. VI, No. 114, November 1894, p. 333.

son apparently moving it. As far as we know there is nothing between the hand stretched out to the table and the surface of the table itself to help the person move it. There is no 'stream of force', like an electric field, that one can imagine connecting the two places as when one directs something by remote radio control. There is no connecting 'matter', as when one moves something with a fishing-rod, for example.

We are quite right to get this feeling, of course. It is a perfectly realistic one. We cannot conceive how such 'action at a distance' is possible. But equally we cannot conceive how action with contact is possible. We may think we can, but this is only because our everyday experience of 'pushing' and 'pulling' things makes us 'familiar' with the process, i.e. it induces a certain state of mind in us. But it does not follow that this state of mind is a realistic one, or is a faithful mirror of reality—or indeed desirable in any way.

If psychokinesis rather than 'pushing' and 'pulling' was the normal mode of interaction with their environment for human beings they might very well become just as 'familiar' with this process as they are now with pushing and pulling.

As a matter of fact, I am sure that if we all woke up tomorrow and found that we could only bring our bodies to within six inches of any other physical object, whereupon it moved just as if we had touched it—then we should very quickly get used to the idea and have no difficulty in 'picking up' objects without breaking them, and so forth.

There is nothing sacrosanct about the surface of our bodies as a boundary to the efficacy of our volition. It is quite conceivable that the limit might have been set elsewhere—say, six inches from the skin, as we have suggested. Let us try to imagine this situation in more detail. To push an object you would have to bring the tip of your finger to within six inches of the object; you would then experience a feeling of resistance—at any rate you would not be able to bring your finger any closer to the object; but if you tried hard enough to bring it closer you would then perceive the object to move. If this happened in ordinary life you would say that it was 'a manifestation of PK'. But if it was the normal way of moving things you would probably not be in the least surprised by it—any more than you are surprised that your arm rises when you wish to lift it. Both phenomena, of course, are equally inexplicable.

As Kant observed, it is just as inconceivable that I should be able to move my arm as that I should be able to move the moon in its orbit. It is merely that you are familiar with the phenomenon of 'moving your arm'. Your arm has responded to your volition so often in the past and with such unvarying reliability that you have come to expect it to do so in the future, and you do not experience any surprise if it does move. But you cannot give any reason why it should move when you want it to, any more than you can explain why the moon should *not* move when you want it to. If you doubt this, consider what you would do if you suddenly found that your arm no longer responded to your volition. You would have no idea what to do, other than to seek outside help. You might have no idea why you could no longer move your arm as you used to. Someone might have surreptitiously injected you with curare, or you might have had an unexpected stroke. Unless you happened to know the symptoms of these conditions you could not tell which had happened to you. Certainly mere introspection could not help you decide which.

As a matter of fact our arm sometimes does fail to move when we intend it to, as when we have been lying on it and it has 'gone to sleep'. Here we go through all the same motions internally that normally precede movement but we observe that the arm does not move. We could not have predicted that it would not—unless of course we have *inferred* that it will not from the feeling of pins and needles that we felt in it, but here again we are only making a probabilistic judgement on the basis of our past experience; we have often observed that pins and needles are associated with paralysis.

Again we could not *teach* a child how to move its arms and legs. How would we set about telling it what to do? Presumably each person learns for himself by trial and error. He observes that certain movements are preceded by certain internal events, though he cannot see why they should be and he could not have predicted it in advance.

Even when we grow up we cannot give any reason why such-and-such an internal event should be followed by such-and-such a bodily movement. Presumably the mental events that precede my voluntarily moving my arm to the right are different from those that precede my voluntarily moving it to the left, but science cannot give me any reason why the mental events preceding my moving it to the right should not have been found to precede it moving to the left, and *vice versa*. Thus, we know no reason why it should not happen that everyone woke up tomorrow morning and found that whenever they intended to move their arm to the right it actually moved to the left and *vice versa*.

❧

It is interesting to compare a person's control

of his normal, physical body with the control which an 'out-of-the-body' subject has over his temporary, ecsomatic 'body'. Here is an example of the latter type of control:

I came out of my body, during the night, & saw my body asleep in the bed, on two occasions. I didn't know what was happening, & so got rather frightened, especially when I realised I only had to look at something & want to approach it, for me to start moving in that direction. I didn't have to put one foot in front of another. I just glided, in the upright position. It was the acceleration which frightened me. I was in the maternity ward at a hospital, & can't remember if I was about to have my child, or whether he was born, but I remember thinking 'I will see if hearing & sight are as acute, out of the body, as in. I moved (glided) to a patient's bed, & listened to the breathing, & thought 'I could hear a pin drop, & yet my physical ears are in the bed.'

It was the weightlessness, which amazed me. I began to wonder what it would be like to go through the ward door. As I looked at the door handle, I found myself moving towards it, gathering speed so rapidly, I got frightened. I thought 'If I go out of that door, I may not find the way back', & with that fear, I snapped backwards, as though flipped by elastic until snap I was back in my body & one with it.

A subject may be able to control his 'body' perfectly well in an out-of-the-body state. He may not be able to tell you how he does it; he may say that he merely 'willed' it to do certain things and found that it did them. But neither can we say how we lift our arm in the normal state. We just do it. And if we are asked how we know that our arm will rise the next time we decide to lift it, we are unable to give any theoretical justification for our belief that it will; we merely expect that it will because of the number of times it has done so in the past.

Similarly, if you suddenly found that you were able to move external objects just by ordering them about, like the man in H. G. Wells's short story who found he could do miracles, you would not be able to give any logical or theoretical reason why this should have happened, nor why it should not have happened earlier than it did. You cannot now give any reason why it should not happen to you tomorrow. You might suddenly develop a gift, like Eusapia Palladino.

Of course, you may say: 'But we have a perfectly satisfactory theory of why an object moves when we push it, but there is no theory at all of how an object could move when a finger is brought within six inches of it.' Actually, this is not true. Ultimately it is equally inconceivable why something should move with contact as it is that it should move without contact. Suppose you start trying to explain how something moves when you push it. You will find yourself talking of positive and negative electric charge, and so on. But the concept of contact breaks down here. Can we say that two electrons are 'touching' when they repel each other? Certainly in the ordinary everyday sense we cannot. An electron does not have a 'solid edge' like an everyday object. And why like charge should repel like, or even why there should apparently be two forms of electricity, is equally inexplicable at the present time as how Eusapia Palladino was able to move tables and chairs without touching them.

All we can say at the present time is that we can *go a little further* in explaining how one moves an object with contact than one can in explaining how one moves an object without contact as Eusapia did. But this is just a statement about the level of knowledge of the human race at a particular point in time. It is a historical or anthropological statement if you like. It does not tell us anything about the fundamental nature of the universe, such as which form of movement—with or without contact—is the more fundamental, or whether one form of movement may ultimately be explained in terms of the other. Least of all does it tell us that only one form of movement is 'logically' or theoretically possible.

PART TWO

VI

Birth Order and Extra-sensory Perception

In this chapter we shall discuss some experiments carried out by the Institute of Psychophysical Research on birth order and extra-sensory perception, that is to say, on the performance of people born in different positions in the family at various card-guessing tasks.

But first, let us try and explain the rationale behind these experiments, i.e. why should one think of looking for a difference between different birth order groups in an ESP situation in the first place?

The first person to study the effect of birth order on personality was Sir Francis Galton, in 1874.[1] His subjects were eminent scientists, mostly members of the Royal Society, and he found that there were more eldest and only

---

[1] Sir Francis Galton, *English Men of Science*, 1874.

sons among them than would be expected by chance.

Galton explained his results by reference to the law of primogeniture: the eldest son was more likely to inherit the financial means that would enable him to achieve eminence in the sphere of his choice. However, he also added that the eldest son was more likely to be given responsibility by his parents at an early age and treated as an equal by them.

Thirty years later Havelock Ellis[1] confirmed Galton's findings in a survey of 975 eminent men and 55 eminent women from all periods of English history. Ellis took as his criterion of eminence the fact of having three or more pages devoted to one's name in the *Dictionary of National Biography*. Again, he found that a far higher proportion of his subjects were eldest or only children than would have occurred by chance.

What Ellis also noticed was that being the youngest child in the family was likewise a favourable condition for success in later life. It was not as favourable as being born an eldest or only child, but it was more favourable than any intermediate position. This fact certainly seems to support the second and more psychological of

---

[1] Havelock Ellis, *A Study of British Genius*, Hurst & Blackett, London, 1904.

Galton's suggested explanations rather than the first. It is hard to see how youngest children could ever have enjoyed any particular economic advantage over their older siblings, at least in a sufficiently high proportion of cases to make them disproportionately successful in later life. On the other hand, it is easy to imagine that the youngest child in a family, like Benjamin in the Old Testament, might tend to be treated differently from his older siblings.

Since the time of Ellis's study the correlation between birth order and success in later life has been found in many different studies, in different parts of the world, and with different groups of people.[1]

That it is not just an I.Q. effect—the eldest children in a family tending for some reason to have more innate ability than later children—is suggested by experiments carried out by Schachter.[2] Schachter found, for example, that when undergraduates were sitting in a waiting-room imminently expecting an unpleasant experience, the eldest and only children showed

---

[1] For a review of the literature, and a discussion of birth order in relation to intelligence, college attendance and personality, see William D. Altus, 'Birth Order and its Sequelae', *Science*, Vol. 151, 1966, pp. 44-9.

[2] S. Schachter, *The Psychology of Affiliation*, Stanford University Press, 1959.

more anxiety and were more likely to want to associate with other people than were undergraduates born in later positions in the family.

I would suggest the following explanation of this experiment. The first-born child is usually the only one in the family who ever has the experience of being the sole object of his parents' attention, without having to compete for it with other siblings. As a result, he is more in the habit of treating his own wants and needs as having importance, and he is less used to subordinating them, or having to subordinate them, to social considerations such as the conflicting requirements of other people. He is more inclined to give his subjective wants priority simply because he is more used to having them treated as important by other people, more specifically his parents.

I think it would be a mistake to infer from Schachter's experiments that the first-born are simply more sociable and extraverted than later-born children, or more dependent on the reassurance and moral support of others for their psychological well-being. Schachter[1] has found, for example, that first-born children tended to be less popular among their undergraduate colleagues than were later-born children.

---

[1] S. Schachter, *Journal of Abnormal and Social Psychology*, Vol. 68, 1964, p. 453.

I would suggest, rather, that the first-born children were simply more 'realistic' about the unpleasantness of the situation in which they found themselves in Schachter's waiting-room than their later-born colleagues. I do not say that they actually had stronger feelings of anxiety, or that the younger children simply 're-pressed' their anxiety, although something like this may have been the case, since Schachter found that the eldest and only children did score more highly on all the questionnaire measures of anxiety he used. What I would primarily suggest is that the first-born were more inclined to treat the anxiety they felt as having importance, and therefore thought it worth communicating to other people. The later-born, in contrast, were more used to having to 'suffer in silence', so to speak, and therefore tended to do so in this experiment.

Now we are not going to suggest that the different personality structure of the first-born child makes him actually better at ESP in some absolute sense than later-born children—although of course he may be, for all we know. What we propose is that the first-born child may simply react differently to a card-guessing situation from later-born children, just as he reacted differently in Schachter's experiment, and that this difference in attitude or reaction will be reflected in his card-guessing score.

That is to say, in any given card-guessing experiment the first-born may, as a group, get more correct guesses than later-born children, or they may get less, but at any rate we expect there will be a significant difference between them.

One reason why one does not wish to assert that in all ESP experiments first-born children will score better, or worse, than later-born children is that the conditions of different experiments will tend to be different, and the first-born children may tend to react favourably to some experimental conditions and unfavourably to others. Similarly, the different personality structures or attitudes of the later-born children may lead them to do well under some conditions and badly under others. In fact, the later-born children may sometimes do well under just those conditions that the first-born find inimical, and *vice versa*. In other words, 'one man's meat is another man's poison' may apply to different birth-order groups in ESP experiments.

꿁

Let us now consider the first of our experiments, which we shall refer to as the *Queen* experiment.[1]

---

[1] The results of this experiment were first reported in C. E. Green, M.E. Eastman and S. T. Adams, 'Birth Order, Family Size and Extra-Sensory Perception',

This experiment consisted of a short ESP test and questionnaire incorporating questions on birth order, which were published in *Queen* Magazine for 29th January, 1964. The subjects were required to guess the nature of 25 randomly chosen Zener cards, each bearing one of the five symbols: star, circle, cross, wavy lines, and square. This series had been prepared by means of random number tables by Professor H. H. Price, who kept the cards, enclosed in sealed opaque envelopes, locked up in a cupboard in his house in Oxford for the duration of the experiment. He was the only person to know the correct order of the cards during that time. The subjects, the readers of *Queen* Magazine, were told that the 25 cards constituted an open series, that is to say, they were chosen from a theoretically infinite number of Zener cards of all kinds, so that there might be more or less than five cards of each symbol. In other words, the series was not made up simply by randomizing the order of a standard pack of 25 Zener cards, which contains five of each symbol.

Three prizes, each consisting of a £5 book token, were offered to the three subjects making the highest direct ESP score, to encourage people to take part in the experiment. The experi-

British Journal of Social and Clinical Psychology, Vol. 5, 1966, pp. 150-2.

ment remained open for three weeks from the date of publication of *Queen* Magazine, and in that time 756 entries were received.

Concerning the practical application of the birth order categories: in classifying subjects as 'eldest', 'only' or 'younger' the overriding criterion was whether the person had ever had the experience of being the only child in the family, at least for a period of time. Thus the elder of a pair of twins, identical or otherwise, was not counted as a 'first born' child. Even if he claimed to have been born first he could obviously never have had the experience of being the sole object of his parents' attention in the way that an only or non-twin eldest child may have. This does not mean of course that all twins had to be left out of the analysis. A member of a pair of twins which had one or more older siblings simply counted as a 'younger' child, whether he was the first or the second of the twins to be born.

Again, any subject who alluded to adopted, half- or step-sibs in a way that cast doubt on his claim to occupy a particular birth order position was omitted. This is not to say that it is impossible for someone with older step- or half-sibs to have what is effectively the same psychological experience as a proper eldest child. For example, Freud was his mother's first child, although his father had two older sons by a previous wife who died. And Freud seems to have received, and indeed been aware of, the special treatment that tends to be accorded to a normal first-born. He later wrote, 'A man who has been the indisputable favourite of his mother keeps for life the feeling of a conqueror, that confidence of success that often induces real success.'[1] However, it is not usually possible to ascertain what has been the childhood experience of such a subject merely from the data given on a questionnaire. He is therefore best omitted from the analysis.

For similar reasons we omitted any 'eldest' child who mentioned that he was preceded by a still-born sibling or one who died before he was born.

Let us now consider the results of this experiment.

Three scoring positions were taken into account: a direct (0) score, or the number of correct guesses the subject made of the card he was consciously aiming at; a forwardly displaced (+1) score, or the number of 'hits' on the target card one ahead of the card the subject was consciously aiming at, and a backwardly displaced (−1) score, or the number of hits on the card

---

[1] Quoted in Ernest Jones, *Sigmund Freud, Life & Work*, Vol. 1, The Hogarth Press, London, 1956, p. 6.

one behind the card he was consciously aiming at.[1]

We had predicted before the experiment began that the eldest and only children, taken as a group, would score significantly differently from the rest. In the event, the eldest and only children scored differently from each other, as well as scoring differently from the rest. In the (—1) position the average score of the eldest and only children, taken together, was 5.16 correct guesses; this is not significantly different from the average score of the younger children, which was 5.11. However, if we consider the three groups, eldest, only and the rest separately from each other, we find that the eldest (excluding only) scored 5.50, the only children 4.70, and the rest 5.11. This difference is highly significant; $p < 0.001$ (as determined by an Analysis of Variance). This probability value must be multiplied by 3 to allow for the fact that three possible scoring positions, (0), (+1), and (—1), were taken into account, but even after this has been done the odds against the result occurring by chance are more than 300 to 1.

ᐂ⊕ᐂ

After the *Queen* experiment had been ar-

---

[1] Cf. S. G. Soal & F. Bateman, *Modern Experiments in Telepathy*, Faber and Faber, London, 1954.

ranged, but before it had yet appeared in *Queen* Magazine, the Institute received the opportunity to conduct a similar experiment in the *Daily Mirror*. This was published on 30th January, 1964, and as the *Queen* experiment was still in progress, the same target series was used for the *Mirror* experiment, i.e. the *Mirror* readers also attempted to guess the order of the 25 cards locked up in Professor Price's cupboard.

It was predicted that any birth order effects would be less marked in the population of lower socio-economic status (the *Mirror* readership) than in the population of higher socio-economic status (the *Queen* readership). This prediction was made in the belief that the differential treatment of the first-born may be less likely to occur in lower-middle and working-class families than in middle class ones.[1]

The prediction was borne out, as the differences between the various birth order groups in the *Mirror* population are not statistically significant in any of the three scoring positions. (See table on p. 81.)

---

[1] Glass *et al.* have suggested that socio-economic factors may explain conflicting birth order results. See D. C. Glass, M. Horwitz, I. Firestone and J. Grinker, 'Birth Order and Reactions to Frustration,' *Journal of Abnormal and Social Psychology*, Vol. 66, No. 2, 1963, pp. 192-4.

The Institute's other experiments, with the exception of the *Isis* experiment, were all carried out with groups of subjects at meetings of university clubs or societies, and were accompanied by a lecture on ESP. As these experiments were for the most part very like one another, I shall describe one of them in detail, the one carried out at Keele University, and then indicate in what respects each of the others differed from it.

The Keele experiment took place at a meeting of the Psychology Society, Keele University. The subjects were for the most part undergraduates, although there were also a few senior members of the University present.

The experiment took place in a large lecture hall of the University. After an introductory talk, one of the officers of the Society, a female undergraduate, who had agreed before the meeting to act as Agent, left the hall and took up a prearranged position at a table in a passage outside. The Experimenter, one of the Institute's Research Officers, remained in the lecture hall throughout the experiment, facing the audience, at one end of the hall.

The Agent was able to hear the instructions of the Experimenter through a partly open door which communicated between the passage and the lecture hall. This door was located at the Experimenter's end of the hall, and the Agent's table was some yards away from this door on the passage side, so that it was impossible for any member of the audience, or the Experimenter, to see the Agent or any part of her, or any part of the table at which she was sitting.

The Agent did not speak at any time throughout the experiment or communicate auditorily in any way with the Experimenter or the subjects.

The target series for this experiment was a binary one, consisting of two of the Zener symbols, 'star' and 'cross'. The series was randomized by tossing a coin, a method suggested by Mr. B. Babington-Smith of the Institute of Experimental Psychology, Oxford University. The target series prepared in this way again constituted an open series, as there is obviously no guarantee that after having tossed a coin a hundred times you will find you have obtained an equal number of 'heads' and 'tails'. The subjects were told what method had been used to produce the target series and that there was not necessarily an equal number of each symbol in the target series as a whole, or, *a fortiori*, in any particular run of 25 cards.

The target series was prepared by a third party in Oxford prior to the experiment, and was taken by the Experimenter to Keele in a sealed opaque envelope. This envelope was only opened by the Agent after she had taken up her position outside the hall at the start of the experiment. Thus the Experimenter had no normal knowledge of the target series until after the guessing was completed. The only people to have any normal knowledge of the target order while the guessing was in progress were the Agent and of course the person in Oxford who had randomized the target series.

When the Agent was in position at her table and the audience were ready to start making their guesses, the Experimenter signalled to the Agent to turn up and look at the first target by calling out 'One', and the audience made their first guess. The subjects wrote down their guesses on duplicated score-sheets, and the Agent wrote down what had been the first target card on a similar sheet.

When the Experimenter judged that all the members of the audience had finished making their first guess, she called out 'Two', the Agent turned up the second card of the target series and wrote down what it was on her form, and the audience likewise made their second guess.

This procedure continued until the audience had made a total of 100 guesses. There were pauses for rest after every 25 guesses, i.e. three pauses in all, breaking the experiment up into four runs of 25 guesses.

In this experiment the eldest children had an average (+1) ESP score of 48.33, the only children an average (+1) score of 47.21, and the rest an average (+1) score of 45.84. An Analysis of Variance carried out on the three groups 'eldest', 'only' and 'the rest', similar to that carried out on the *Queen* data, yields significant results. (See table on p. 81.)

~∞~

The *Isis* experiment was similar to the Queen experiment, the target series consisting of an open series of 25 Zener cards, of all five denominations. The experiment was published in the Oxford undergraduate magazine *Isis* for 2nd June, 1966.

The remaining experiments resembled the Keele experiment. The Oxford University Graduate Society experiment differed from the others in that the audience consisted of persons of all ages and not mainly of undergraduates, the members of this society being former undergraduates of the University who happened to be still living in or near Oxford. Also, in this experiment the target series was not a binary one, but consisted of an open series of 100 Zener cards of all five denominations.

In the Imperial College experiment and the

second experiment with the Oxford University Society for Psychical Research an attempt was made systematically to vary the conditions under which the subjects made their guesses to see whether it affected different birth order groups in different ways. In the Imperial College experiment the variable manipulated was whether or not the subject could see the Experimenter. The Experimenter was in a different room from the subjects, and for half the guesses a closed-circuit television system was switched on, so that the subjects could see the Experimenter as well as hear her instructions over an Intercom. For the remaining guesses only the Experimenter's voice was audible, giving the signal to make each guess. The Agent was in a third room, adjacent to the Experimenter's room but out of her sight. The subjects started by making 10 guesses under the 'non-visual' condition, and then made 10 guesses under the 'visual' condition, the two conditions alternating every 10 guesses until a total of 50 guesses had been made under each condition. The second experiment with the Oxford University Society for Psychical Research was similar except that for half the guesses music was played while the subjects made their guesses, and for half the guesses no music was played.

As the object of these experiments was deliberately to manipulate the conditions so as to produce an effect on the subjects' ESP scores, the two conditions are treated separately for the purpose of the birth order analysis.

The results of all these experiments are summarized in the table on p. 81.

The last entry concerns an experiment carried out by Margaret E. Eastman, then a Research Officer of the Institute, while on a Fellowship in Parapsychology at the Department of Psychology, City College, New York. In this experiment the eldest children again scored best at the ESP task, while the only children scored very much like the rest. An Analysis of Variance on the three groups' scores gives odds against chance of more than 100 to 1. Margaret Eastman remarks that, as undergraduate students at City College, her subjects were 'probably from mainly Jewish middle and lower-middle class homes'.[1]

Except for the last entry, concerning Margaret Eastman's City College experiment, each of the p-values in the last column of the table should be multiplied by three to allow for the fact that three different scoring positions were taken into account. Margaret Eastman's experi-

---

[1] Margaret E. Eastman, 'The Relationship of ESP Scores to Knowledge of Target Location, and to Birth Order and Family Size', M.A. Thesis, City College, New York, 1966, p. 30.

	Scoring position	Eldest		Only		Younger		Analysis of Variance p-value
		No. of subjects	Mean ESP score	No. of subjects	Mean ESP score	No. of subjects	Mean ESP score	
Queen	(−1)	220	5·50	162	4·70	333	5·11	<0·001
Daily Mirror	(+1)	1454	4·98	812	4·94	2789	4·85	<0·2
Oxford University Graduate Society	(0)	11	13·27	10	16·00	15	16·93	<0·05
Imperial College of Science and Technology, University of London — Visual Condition	(0)	57	25·00	26	24·35	66	24·11	>0·2
Non-visual Condition	(0)	57	25·75	26	24·89	66	25·26	>0·2
University of Keele	(+1)	89	48·33	39	47·21	88	45·84	<0·01
Oxford University Society for Psychical Research—I	(+1)	29	19·31	13	17·77	25	18·16	<0·2
Isis	(0)	87	4·69	54	5·50	95	5·22	<0·05
Oxford University Society for Psychical Research—II — Music Condition	(0)	31	24·84	17	23·77	45	26·16	<0·05
Silent Condition	(0)	31	25·87	17	24·59	45	24·76	>0·2
City College, New York	(0)	28	22·14	25	18·76	60	19·08	<0·01

ment is an exception, since in this case only one scoring position, the direct (0) position, was considered.

~⊕~

One interesting feature to emerge from these experiments is the role of the only children. The only children are the 'floating voters', so to speak; sometimes they vote with the eldest children, as in the Keele experiment; at other times they vote with 'the rest', as in Margaret Eastman's experiment at City College; or again, they may decide to form a party of their own that is different from both the eldest and the younger children, as in the *Queen* experiment.

What are the reasons for this difference between the eldest and only children?

There is of course one very big difference between the childhood experiences of eldest and only children. The only child remains an only child all his life, whereas the eldest child finds he has to compete for the attention of his parents with other, younger children as soon as a younger sibling is born. Psychoanalysts, of course, regard this experience as extremely important. The older child is supposed to be extremely jealous of the newcomer, who has, at least to some extent, supplanted him in the attentions of his mother. Whether one believes this or not, it is obvious that having one or more younger siblings might make for considerable differences in the childhood experience of eldest and only children, which might tend to affect their personality and attitudes in later life.

There is in fact independent evidence for personality differences between eldest and only children. Schachter,[1] for example, found that only children made more successful fighter pilots than eldest children. First-born children were on the whole much less successful as pilots than younger children, but of the few first-born children who did 'make the grade', so to speak, a disproportionate number were only children rather than first-born children with younger siblings.

Again, Schwartzman[2] found that in a learning task eldest children with one or more younger siblings were more responsive than only children to 'social reinforcement' for correct answers. (The social reinforcement took the form of encouraging utterances from the experimenter such as 'Good', 'That's fine', etc.) Schwartz-

---

[1] Schachter, *The Psychology of Affiliation*, op. cit., pp. 72-7.

[2] S. Schwartzman, 'Birth Order and Social Conditioning: a Study of the Relationship between the Position of a Child in his Family and Responsivity to Social Conditioning', *Dissertation Abstracts*, Vol. 23, 1962, pp. 2222-3.

man predicted this result on the grounds that the only child, never having had to share the attention of his parents with any other child, would tend to be more 'satiated' with social reinforcement than the eldest child with one or more younger siblings. He reasoned that the less satiated eldest children would be more responsive to the sort of attention of which they had been at least partially deprived in childhood, compared with the only children, who had never had to share their parents' encouragement with other siblings. We might compare this with the way in which a group of hungry subjects might improve their learning performance more in response to rewards of food for correct answers than a group of subjects who had just had a good meal and were relatively uninterested in food.

Although we deliberately did not predict which of the birth order groups would tend to do best at the ESP task, it is interesting that, in the event, in the three most significant experiments it was the eldest children who did best. Of course, it still does not follow that the eldest children are 'the best at ESP' in any absolute sense, or even that they will always do better than the other birth order groups in card-guessing experiments. However, the eldest do seem to have been particularly successful in the most significant of the experiments carried out so far, and it will be interesting to see whether this relationship holds with other groups of subjects, tested by different experimenters.

VII

The Marquis d'Hervey de Saint-Denys

In this chapter we shall discuss the experiences of a habitual lucid dreamer, the Marquis d'Hervey de Saint-Denys, and compare them with the experiences of other habitual lucid dreamers, notably those discussed by Celia Green in her book *Lucid Dreams*.[1]

The Marquis d'Hervey de Saint-Denys was born in 1822, and started to take an interest in his dreams at the age of 13. He was educated at home, and used to occupy some of his spare time in drawing and sketching. 'One day,' he writes, 'I had the idea ... of sketching from memory scenes from a strange dream which had made a vivid impression on me. I was pleased with the result, and soon had a special album for portraying the scenes and figures of my dreams. Each drawing was accompanied by a

---

[1] Hamish Hamilton, 1968.

detailed explanation of the circumstances which had led up to or followed the image in the dream.' (pp. 58-9)[1] In the course of the next five years the Marquis filled a total of 22 exercise books with accounts and sketches of his dreams.

His first lucid dream occurred after he had been keeping a journal of his dreams for 207 days, and arose as follows:

As a result of thinking about my dreams during the day, and analysing and describing them, these activities became part of the store of memories of waking life on which my mind drew during sleep. Thus one night I dreamt that I was writing up my dreams, some of which were particularly unusual. On waking, I thought what a great pity it was that I had not been aware of this exceptional situation while still asleep. What a golden opportunity lost!—I thought. I would have been able to note so many interesting details. I was obsessed by this idea for several days, and the mere fact that I kept thinking about it during the day soon resulted in my having the same dream again. There was one modification,

---

[1] Unless otherwise indicated, all the quotations in this chapter are from Hervey de Saint-Denys's book, *Les Rêves et les Moyens de les Diriger*, first published in 1867 by Amyat, Paris, and reprinted in 1964 by the Cercle du Livre Précieux, Paris. The page references given in brackets after each quotation refer to the 1964 edition. The translations are by myself.

however: this time the original ideas summoned up by association the idea that I was dreaming, and I became perfectly aware of this fact. I was able to concentrate particularly on the details of the dream that interested me, so as to fix them in my mind all the more clearly on waking. (p. 69)

Like a number of other subjects, Hervey de Saint-Denys found that the frequency of his lucid dreams increased with practice, so to speak. His second lucid dream did not occur until a week after his first. But six months later he was having lucid dreams on an average of two nights out of five, and by the end of a year, on three nights out of four.

Hervey de Saint-Denys remarks that the tendency to have lucid dreams increases or diminishes according to the amount of effort or attention one puts into having them. While he was keeping a daily journal of his dreams, that is, between the ages of thirteen and eighteen, he achieved lucidity practically every night; whereas at the time of writing his book, more than twenty years later, he was only doing so approximately every other night. However, he suggests that once the ability to have lucid dreams has been acquired, one never loses it entirely, and can increase their frequency whenever one pays attention to doing so.

Hervey de Saint-Denys also believed that almost anybody can have lucid dreams who wants them. He mentions that out of fourteen people with whom he discussed the possibility of lucid dreams, and who were willing to follow his instructions, only one failed entirely to have a lucid dream despite serious efforts. Two had had occasional lucid dreams already and another nine succeeded 'very quickly' in having them (p. 396).

In interpreting these results we must bear in mind, of course, that the Marquis's sample may not have been representative of the population at large. The Marquis was a Professor of Tartaro-Manchu at the Collège de France, and the fourteen subjects were presumably drawn from among his personal and professional acquaintances, although he does not give us any particulars about them.

❦

Hervey de Saint-Denys does not seem ever to have had a lucid dream starting from the waking state, like Ouspensky, although he came very close to doing so on occasion. The following is an example in which Hervey de Saint-Denys was able to trace the antecedents of a lucid dream back to the moment of falling asleep. Incidentally, Ouspensky's lucid dreams starting from the waking state occurred in the morning after he had already woken up and fallen asleep again, whereas the following lucid dream of Hervey de Saint-Denys's seems to have occurred first thing after falling asleep at night.

I have just forced myself awake soon after falling asleep, having had a moment of insight in which I remembered the observations I wished to make, and thought it would be useful to write down my results straight away. First of all I was feeling drowsy and was thinking in a highly confused way of the people who had been dining with us this evening, and in particular of the pretty face of Mme. de S——. I could not make out her face distinctly at first, but then it became clearer. Then without my knowing how this came about, I found I was looking, not at her, but at her cousin, Mme. L——, seated in front of a tapestry-frame. She was working on a picture of a garland of fruit and flowers, full of admirable shading. I could see every detail of the work quite distinctly, as well as every feature of the room and of Mme. de S——'s costume. At that moment I suddenly realised I was dreaming, and that I had only just fallen asleep. I forced myself awake by an effort of will, and, taking up my pencil, I immediately made this note . . . (p. 229)

Hervey de Saint-Denys's lucid dreams, like those of other habitual lucid dreamers, seem to have achieved a high degree of perceptual realism, at least on occasion. Here, for example, is part of a lucid dream in which he carefully examines a part of his visual environment:

I felt fast asleep. I could see clearly all the little objects which decorate my study. My attention alighted on a porcelain tray, in which I keep my pencils and pens, and which has some very unusual decoration on it. In reality this tray has never been broken in any way. I suddenly thought: Whenever I have seen this tray in waking life, it has always been in one piece. What if I were to break it in my dream? How would my imagination represent the broken tray? I immediately broke it in pieces. I picked up the pieces and examined them closely. I observed the sharp edges of the lines of breakage, and the jagged cracks which split the decorative figures in several places. I had seldom had such a vivid dream. (p. 275)

In the following example he considers the perceptual quality of his visual experiences in a lucid dream, and experiments with his sense of smell:

I dreamt that I was in a garden walk. I was aware that I was dreaming, and thought of the various problems which I was interested in studying. There was a branch of flowering lilac in front of me. I considered it with genuine attention. I remembered having read that memories of smell are rarely accurate in dreams. I took hold of the branch, and assured myself that the smell of the lilac was indeed summoned up by its association with the related impressions connected with the imaginary, but *voluntary*, act. Now, I said to myself, what I am perceiving is an image of an intact, oblong head of lilac of a particular shape, still connected to its bush. Is this a stereotyped image, the unvarying reproduction of some memory-image engraved on the fibres of my brain, as the materialists would say? In that case, I should be powerless to modify it by my imagination and will. As I made these reflections, I had broken the branch, and I now tore off the lilac head. As I broke off each piece, I noticed how the appearance of the spray, as it became progressively smaller, still remained clearly and precisely what it would have been if I had done this in reality. When there remained no more than a very small cluster of lilac flowers, I wondered: shall I finish this illusory act of destruction, or shall I call a halt at this last modification of the original image? I venture to say that this depended entirely on a free decision on my part. But at that moment I awoke. (pp. 243–244)

In the lucid dream which we have just quoted the Marquis's olfactory experiences, i.e. of smelling the lilac, were apparently realistic and appropriate, that is to say, the same as he would have experienced had he sniffed a head of lilac in waking life. In the following lucid dream he performed a similar experiment with his sense of taste, but the results were more unexpected:

In the background of the dream-scene I saw a street which I recognised as one in Seville, where I had not been for ten years. I immediately remembered that there was a very famous ice-cream shop round the corner of this street. I was curious to know how my memory would acquit itself if I tried guiding my dream in this direction, and set off accordingly. I perceived the shop with minute distinctness, and recognised in it all sorts of little cakes of characteristic shapes. Among the other refreshments were some hazelnut water-ices, something which I had never come across elsewhere. I then reflected that this was a valuable opportunity to see whether I could recall a taste as faithfully as I recalled visual images. I chose one of these imaginary water-ices, and raised it to my lips, concentrating all my attention on tasting it. I realised that my memory had failed me and was only providing me with an approximation to the sensation which was required of it. What it produced was an almond taste, and not a hazel-nut taste. I woke myself immediately by an effort of will, in order to make a note of this. (pp. 257–8)

Hervey de Saint-Denys believed that all dream-images were based on memory-images. Since, in his view, it was impossible in waking life to recall the memory of a pain with anything like the vividness of the original sensation, he considered that it would be impossible to have a realistic sensation of pain during dreams. The following extract from one of his lucid dreams seems to support this view. However, we should bear in mind that not all lucid dreamers agree with it.[1]

I remembered how I had noticed that, by a fortunate dispensation of nature, the memory of a sharp physical pain never impresses itself distinctly on the memory and cannot, in consequence, be revived in dreams. I noticed a bradawl among the collection of objects on my table. As I was perfectly sure that I was dreaming, I took this instrument and plunged it into my hand. My memory immediately presented me with the visual image of a bleeding wound. But there was no pain at all, scarcely even that painful instinctive reaction which the sight of the same wound in another man would certainly have caused in me. (p. 363)

Like other habitual lucid dreamers, Hervey de Saint-Denys was apparently capable of trains of analytical thought in lucid dreams that were as logical as those he carried out in waking life.

In the following lucid dream he discusses the left leads to some kind of ruined manor. I with himself the problem of free will and its relationship to dreaming, and carries out an experiment on this subject while still asleep.

... I dreamt that I was out riding in fine weather. I became aware of my true situation,

---

[1] Cf. p. 112, and Celia Green, *Lucid Dreams*, op. cit., p. 75.

and remembered the question of whether or not I could exercise free will in controlling my actions in a dream. 'Well now,' I said to myself, 'This horse is only an illusion; this countryside that I am passing through is merely stage-scenery. But even if I have not evoked these images by conscious volition, I certainly seem to have some control over them. I decide to gallop, I gallop; I decide to stop, I stop. Now here are two roads in front of me. The one on the right appears to plunge into a dense wood; the one on feel quite distinctly that I am free to turn either right or left, and so to decide for myself whether I wish to produce images relating to the ruins or images relating to the wood.' I began by taking the righthand road, but then it occurred to me that as this was such a clear dream it would be more interesting from the experimental point of view to dream of riding past the turrets and keep of the manor. I could then try to memorise the principal details of the architecture, and see if, when I awoke, I could recognise the memories on which they had been based. I therefore took the left-hand path, and dismounted by a picturesque drawbridge. For some time I very attentively examined numerous details of the manor's architecture: ogival arches, carved masonry, half-corroded pieces of iron-work, and fissures and alterations in the wall. I admired the minute precision with which all this was portrayed. However, while I was still studying the gigantic lock of a dilapidated old door, everything suddenly faded and became blurred, like the figures of a diorama when it goes out of fo-

cus. I felt I was waking up. My eyes opened
onto the real world, and the only light I could
see was that from my night-light. It was three
o'clock in the morning. (pp. 240-1)

The following case provides another illustra-
tion of the sort of analytical thinking which
Hervey de Saint-Denys performed in lucid
dreams:

I found myself in a very elegantly furnished
room. I could distinguish all the furniture perfectly clearly, although I could not recall the
source of the memory-images on which it was
based. At the same time I said to myself that my
imagination could not have instantaneously in-
vented so many minute details. I saw a mirror in
front of me, and looked at myself in it. I saw I
was wearing a dressing-gown with a peculiar flo-
ral design. I recognised this as the design of a
roll of material which I had admired the day before in the window of a large shop. I thought to
myself: this image is evidently the result of a
combination of memories; the shape is derived
from my memory of some dressing-gown or
other, and the appearance of the material from a
piece that I have only seen as an opened-out
roll. I reflected upon several other questions
bearing upon the power of the imagination to
combine different memory-images. (p. 363)

The only mental operation with which Hervey de Saint-Denys appears to have had any difficulty in lucid dreams was that of realizing that

his companions were not really sharing his experiences, and were only figments of his imagination. He says that he experienced 'extreme difficulty' in recognizing this fact, even in the most lucid of his lucid dreams. 'For example,' he writes, 'I dreamt that I was visiting the tower of a church with one of my friends, and that we were gazing in wonder at the splendid panorama before us. I knew very well that this was only a dream, but nevertheless I said to the friend who was with me: "Please be sure to remember this dream, so that we can talk about it tomorrow when we are awake." ' (p. 357)

However, this difficulty seems to have arisen from a psychological or emotional resistance to admitting a certain kind of thought to consciousness, rather than from poor intellectual functioning in general.

Incidentally, the Marquis's difficulty seems to be rather idiosyncratic, and not one that is shared by other habitual lucid dreamers. In fact, a number of other subjects seem to find it amusing to tell the characters they meet in lucid dreams that they are only figments of the imagination, however realistic they may appear. An example of this is provided by the dream quoted in Chapter 1, p. 19.

~⊶⊷~

Some subjects have found it difficult to

remember correctly in lucid dreams the immediate circumstances of their lives, such as where
they were sleeping or their plans for the next
day. This seems to be the result of a type of
censorship arising from an emotional resistance,
rather than of any intellectual deficiency.[1] In
the following dream, however, Hervey de
Saint-Denys is able to remember his plans for
the following day, and judges correctly where
he is sleeping, although this latter judgement
seems to be more the result of a conscious
deduction than a spontaneous memory.

I dreamt that I was in the country. (In reality
I was in Paris.) I was receiving a visit from a
friend. The countryside was green, and the trees
were wearing their summer foliage. However, as
in the last dream [the one about taking medicine, see p. 104], I found myself very preoccupied with a certain idea. This was that I wished
to get up at six o'clock in the morning to go and
meet my sister, who was returning after a rather
long absence. There was nothing surprising
about the visit of my friend which I dreamt I
was receiving in the countryside. I was therefore
able to accept without astonishment the scenes
which presented themselves before me. But the
thoughts kept recurring to me that I was expecting my sister, that it was in Paris and not in the

---

[1] Cf. Celia Green, *Lucid Dreams*, op. cit., p. 86ff. and
p. 91ff.

country that she was due to arrive, and that we were in the middle of winter and not summer. I reflected that everything that I seemed to be seeing could only be a dream and that I was quite certainly asleep. At that moment I heard five o'clock strike, and counted the five strokes. That proved to me that I was indeed in Paris, where I live next to a church with a rather noisy clock. I also concluded that I still had an hour in which to sleep. Not letting my mind dwell on an order of ideas which might lead to my waking up, I instead concentrated all my attention on the images which my imagination had evoked. I identified myself with the situation which it had created; I walked in the sun with the friend who was visiting me; in short, I calmly continued with my dream. (pp. 256-7)

It is possible of course that the bells which the Marquis heard in his dream were entirely hallucinatory, despite the fact that he apparently recognized them as being the bells of the neighbouring church. That is to say, it may be that the church clock was not actually striking at that moment, and that it was not really five o'clock. The Marquis may have merely dreamt that they were striking. Hervey de Saint-Denys does not offer us any independent evidence on this point. If we assume that the dream bells did have a basis in reality, then this dream provides the only example I know in which a lucid dream included external stimuli which were recognized as such by the dreamer.

It would be possible to devise an experimental situation for determining whether external stimuli could be incorporated into a lucid dream, and if so, to investigate what forms such incorporation took and whether it differed from the analogous phenomenon when it occurred in non-lucid dreams. In a laboratory situation it would be possible to wake the subject soon after delivering a standard stimulus such as a bell or a knock, and compare his verbal reports when he had been woken from a lucid dream with his verbal reports when he had been woken from a non-lucid dream.

If we accept the Marquis's dream as providing a genuine example of the incorporation of external stimuli into a lucid dream, then it appears that there are differences between this and the analogous phenomenon occurring in non-lucid dreams. In the first place, the Marquis recognized the stimuli as arising from some source external to the dream, whereas it is only retrospectively on waking, if at all, that the subject recognizes the external origin of certain sense-data in non-lucid dreams. Secondly, external stimuli are characteristically 'woven into' the fabric of a non-lucid dream in a way that rationalizes their presence in terms of the current dream. The striking of the bells in the Marquis's lucid dream, however, did not have any rationalization in terms of his dream of being in the countryside—he did not suddenly dream of seeing a clock-tower in the distance, for example.

❧⚙❧

Hervey de Saint-Denys gives the following interesting example of apparent cryptomnesia in a lucid dream, i.e. the incorporation into it of consciously forgotten memories:

I had a very clear, coherent and precise dream of being in Brussels. (In reality I had never been there.) I was walking quietly along a very lively street, flanked by numerous shops whose multi-coloured signs stretched their long arms above the passers-by.

'Now this is very strange,' I said to myself. 'One really cannot suppose that my imagination is inventing all these details. The Orientals believe that while one's body is asleep the mind travels off on its own, but this does not seem to me a hypothesis to which one can give serious consideration either. Nevertheless, although I have never visited Brussels, here I am enjoying a perfect view of the famous church of St. Gudule which I remember seeing in prints. I do not have the slightest recollection of ever walking down a street like this in any town anywhere. If my memory can preserve such minute impressions without my knowledge, this is a fact that deserves to be established. It will certainly be interesting to experiment with this point. The important thing is to have definite data to work with, so I must observe everything very closely.' I immediately started to examine one of the shops with the closest possible attention, so that if I should ever happen to come across it one day in waking life, I should be able to recognise it without any doubt whatever. The shop in front of which I was standing was a hosier's shop, and it was on this that I concentrated my attention. The first thing I noticed about it was that its shop-sign consisted of two crossed arms, one red and the other white, jutting out over the street. These were crowned by an enormous cap of striped cotton. I read the name of the shopkeeper several times so as to be sure to remember it. I noted the number of the house, and also the fact that it had a little door in the shape of an ogive, which was decorated at the top with a number with intertwining numerals. Then I shook myself awake with a violent effort of will—something which is always possible when one is aware that one is dreaming. Before these vivid impressions had time to fade, I hastened to write them down and sketch all the details with great care. (pp. 78-9)

Some months later Hervey de Saint-Denys was able to visit Brussels. There he saw the church of St. Gudule, just as in his lucid dream. But, try as he would, he could not find the street he had dreamt about.

He describes the sequel to this episode as follows:

Several years went by. I had almost forgotten about this episode in my adolescent investigations, when I was obliged to travel through various parts of Germany which I had previously visited in my very earliest childhood. Thus it was that I found myself in Frankfurt, having a quiet cigarette after lunch, and strolling along without any particular destination in mind. I entered the Judengasse and suddenly a whole host of vague and indefinable reminiscences came crowding into my mind. I tried to discover the cause of this strange sensation, and suddenly I remembered the object of my fruitless searches in Brussels. I could no longer see the silhouette of the church of St. Gudule, of course. But this was certainly the street I had sketched in my dream journal. Here were the same whimsical shopsigns, the same crowd of people, the same bustle, which had formerly struck me so vividly in my dream. As I have mentioned, there was one house in particular which I had examined minutely. I could remember its number and external appearance perfectly. I ran to look for it with genuine excitement. Would I meet with a fresh disappointment, or was I at last going to solve one of the most interesting problems I had ever set myself? Imagine my joy and astonishment when I found myself in front of a house so exactly similar to that of my dream that it was almost as if I had gone back six years in time and was still asleep. (pp. 79-80)

The Marquis explains that he had been in Frankfurt once before, three or four years before having the lucid dream. He concludes that he must have been down this street on that occasion, although he did not consciously remember anything about it, either at the time of his dream or when he found the dream street in real life.

~~❦~~

Hervey de Saint-Denys had a considerable degree of control over his lucid dreams.

In the first place, he was able to conjure up fresh scenes just by walking or riding in the appropriate direction. Examples of this process are provided by the dreams already quoted of the ruined manor and of the water-ice.

His second technique for altering the dream scenery consisted of covering his eyes, and willing the appearance of some new scene. Here is his account of the first occasion on which he made use of this procedure. It is interesting to note that he reports working out the technique while already asleep and in the middle of a lucid dream.

... I was asleep and fully aware that I was dreaming. I was watching without much interest the development of a sequence of images of an extremely distinct kind. It occurred to me that I might take advantage of my situation to make some experiments on the extent to which I was able to evoke particular images by will-power alone. I tried to think of a subject on which to concentrate, and remembered the monsters which had frightened me so much in my earlier dreams [see below, p. 102]. I tried to summon them up by remembering them as vividly as possible and willing as strongly as I could to see them again. My first attempt was unsuccessful. I was at that moment looking at a beautiful country landscape gilded by the rays of the sun. In the middle of this scene were some men harvesting, and carts loaded with corn. There was no sign of any monster appearing in response to my summons. My dream showed no signs of altering its tranquil course. At this point, and while still dreaming, I thought: 'A dream is after all a reflection of real life, and even the most incoherent events in dreams follow certain laws, analogous to those which govern the sequence of events in waking life. I mean that if I dream that I have broken my arm, for example, then I will also dream of carrying it in a sling or using it with care. Again, if I dream that someone has closed the shutters of the room I am in, then I will immediately dream that the light has been shut out and that I am in darkness.' As a result of this train of thought it occurred to me that if I put my hand over my eyes while I was dreaming, I should first of all have the illusion that the scene before me had disappeared, just as it would if I covered my eyes in waking life. I thought that if I could once blot out the previous images, it might be easier for me to evoke fresh objects on which to concentrate. I quickly proceeded to experiment along these lines. I put my hand over my eyes and the scene of the countryside at harvest-time, which I had tried in vain to obliterate

by will-power alone, was immediately blotted
out. I then once more summoned up the memory
of the dreadful monsters. This time my mind
was clearly focussed on the required memory,
and the monsters appeared as if by enchant-
ment. The image was clear, brilliant, and tumul-
tuous; and the transition from the former scene
was so sudden that I scarcely had time to consider how it had come about before I awoke.
(pp. 247-8)

Delighted with his discovery, the Marquis
made frequent use of this technique thereafter,
either to banish a disagreeable impression, or to
summon up some fresh image that took his
fancy in the course of a dream. He gives the following proportions of success and failure, or
partial failure, in his attempts. Out of a sample
of 42 attempts, 23 were a complete success, 'that
is to say there was a clear-cut and immediate
substitution of the desired image for the one of
which I wished to rid myself'. On 13 occasions
there was only partial success: 'the unwanted
image disappeared, but the fresh one that took
its place did not correspond exactly to the one
he wanted. On four occasions a rapid association of ideas went through his mind while the
change-over was taking place and he ended up
looking at a completely different scene from the
one he originally intended. On only one occasion was the scene unchanged when he opened

his eyes, and on one occasion he simply woke up.

—◦⊛◦—

Hervey de Saint-Denys believed that one could only dream about things that one had already experienced in waking life, or at least about things whose constituent elements one had already experienced in reality. He therefore believed that it would be impossible to dream of one's own suicide, for example, since obviously one had no memory of this phenomenon on which one's subconscious mind could draw in constructing the dream. To test his hypothesis, he several times threw himself from great heights in lucid dreams, to see what his subconscious mind would produce when confronted with this situation. Here is his account of the first such occasion:

... I dreamt that I was walking along a street. Every feature of my dream was perfectly precise, and yet I was quite aware that I was not awake. I suddenly remembered about the experiment I wished to make. I immediately climbed to the top floor of what seemed to be a very tall house. I looked through an open window at the pavement far below. For a moment I admired the perfect realism of the scene, and then, without allowing the dream time to change, I threw myself from the window, full of anxious curiosity.... I instantly forgot everything that had gone before, and started to dream that I was standing in the square in front of a cathedral. I was among a group of curious passers-by who were thronging round the body of a dead man. The people round me were saying that this unknown man had thrown himself from the tower of the church. I saw them carry away his body on a stretcher. (pp. 249-50)

Hervey de Saint-Denys remarks that he was only able to piece together the sequence of events in this dream on waking, from which I think it is clear that his dream was no longer lucid after the sudden shift of scene to the square of the cathedral, although he does not say so explicitly.

He remarks that on each occasion on which he repeated the experiment of jumping from a height, a similar sudden shift of ideas occurred at the crucial moment, although in each case the fresh train of ideas was in some way related to what had gone before. For example, on one occasion he dreamt of jumping into a pit, whereupon he suddenly found himself surrounded by magicians and astrologers, all of whom were dressed like a certain astrologer, named Matthew Laensberg. On waking he remembered that this Matthew Laensberg had a reputation for 'letting himself fall into pits'. On another occasion Hervey de Saint-Denys threw himself from a cliff, whereupon he immediately dreamt that he was floating in a balloon.

The following experiment carried out by one of the Institute's own correspondents is in some ways comparable with those of the Marquis:

> I was walking about a large meadow which sloped down towards a main road on which there was traffic. I was saying to myself that 'I am dreaming so let's test this out by jumping under one of those cars'. I ran down the hill and jumped under a car, when I woke.

Hervey de Saint-Denys also considered trying to cut his throat or shoot himself in a lucid dream, but never succeeded in carrying out either of these experiments. On one occasion he got as far as holding a razor in his hand, but he says, 'my instinctive horror of the action I wished to simulate proved stronger than my conscious volition'.

As regards trying to shoot himself, he says that obtaining and operating a pistol in the dream always took so long that his attention was deflected in the meantime from the purpose in hand. One wonders whether this difficulty may not have reflected an unconscious resistance on his part to going through with the test. For example, he writes that on one occasion 'just as I was about to take out my pistols, my attention was drawn by the little bundle of keys among which was the key to my pistol case. This made me notice the key to a drawer in which I remembered putting some photographs. I remembered one of them in particular. The thought of it distracted my attention, and my mind was soon far from the question of pistols.' (pp. 250-1) One wonders whether his mind would have wandered so easily if the task in hand had not been such a conflict-producing one. Certainly on other occasions he seems to have been able to formulate and retain in mind an intention for quite long periods during a lucid dream. For example, one supposes that it must have taken him some time in his dream to climb to the top floor of the house from which he threw himself into the street below, and he even reports being able to pause and admire the view without forgetting his intention in being there.

Hervey de Saint-Denys remarks that unpleasant features tend to be absent from lucid dreams, and that it is sufficient to realize that one is dreaming for any unpleasant feature of a non-lucid dream to lose its nightmarish quality.

Here is an example in which he finally manages to rid himself of a recurrent nightmare by becoming lucid at the crucial moment:

I was not aware that I was dreaming, and imagined I was being pursued by abominable monsters. I was fleeing through an endless series of rooms. I had difficulty in opening the doors that divided them, and no sooner had I closed each door behind me than I heard it opened again by the hideous procession of monsters. They were uttering horrible cries as they tried to catch me. I felt they were gaining on me. I awoke with a start, panting and bathed in sweat.

I do not know how this dream originated. It was probably caused by a physiological disorder on the first occasion. However, it recurred several times in the course of the next six weeks, and on these occasions it was evidently evoked by the mere fact that it had made such an impression on me the first time, and because I had such an instinctive fear of experiencing it again. If I happened to find myself alone in an enclosed room during a dream, I was immediately reminded of this dreadful nightmare. I would glance apprehensively at the door, and the mere thought of the dreaded monsters had precisely the effect of causing them to appear. The same scene, with all its attendant terrors, would then recur exactly as before. Although at that time I was very frequently aware of my state when I was dreaming, by an unfortunate coincidence this awareness was never present when the nightmare situation recurred; and this made it seem all the more unpleasant when I awoke. However, on the fourth occurrence of the nightmare, just as the monsters were about to start pursuing me again, I suddenly became aware of my true situation. My desire to rid myself of these illusory terrors gave me the strength to overcome my fear. I did not flee, but instead, making a great effort of will, I put my back up against the wall, and determined to look the phantom monsters full in the face. This time I would make a deliberate study of them, and not just glance at them, as I had on previous occasions. I must admit that I experienced a fairly violent emotional shock at first. The appearance in dreams of something one has been dreading to see can still have a considerable effect on one's mind, even when one is forewarned against it. I stared at my principal assailant. He bore some resemblance to one of those bristling and grimacing demons which are sculptured on cathedral porches. Academic curiosity soon overcame all my other emotions. I saw the fantastic monster halt a few paces from me, hissing and leaping about. Once I had mastered my fear his actions appeared merely burlesque. I noticed the claws on one of his hands, or paws, I should say. There were seven in all, each very precisely delineated. The monster's features were all precise and realistic: hair and eyebrows, what looked like a wound on his shoulder, and many other details. In fact, I would class this as one of the clearest images I had had in dreams. Perhaps this image was based on a memory of some Gothic bas-relief. Whether this was so or not, my imagination was certainly responsible for the movement and colour in the image. The result of concentrating my attention on this figure was that all his acolytes vanished, as if by magic. Soon the leading monster also began to slow down, lose precision, and take on a downy appearance. He finally changed into a sort of

floating hide, which resembled the faded cos-
tumes used as street-signs by fancy-dress shops at
carnival-time. Some unremarkable scenes followed, and finally I woke up. (pp. 245-247)

～⊛～

Unlike other habitual lucid dreamers, Hervey de Saint-Denys does not seem to have been
prone to 'false awakenings'. At any rate, he does
not mention them as a separate phenomenon.
He describes one false awakening happening at
the end of an experience which resembles an
out-of-the-body experience (see below, p. 105).
In addition, he mentions one dream which
might be said to include a false awakening.
Here is his account of the dream in question:

I was ill, and preoccupied with the thought of
having to take some medicine in the morning.
This preoccupation formed the subject of my
dream. The medicine was placed ready on a table by my bed, and I dreamt that I had just
woken up and was about to drink it. I noticed
that the medicine was in its usual cup. However,
I remembered quite clearly that this cup had
been broken the previous day, and replaced by
one of a quite different shape. I concluded from
this that I was dreaming, and that if I was really
going to take the medicine I should have to
wake up first. However, I reflected that I was
needing sleep, and that I should be sure to wake
up soon enough in any case. I therefore made no

attempt to wake up, and instead I abandoned myself to the illusions of the dream. (p. 256)

:~@~:

Hervey de Saint-Denys reports one experience which should possibly be classified as an out-of-the-body experience rather than a lucid dream:

Last night I dreamt that my soul had left my body, and that I was travelling vast distances with the speed of thought. I first of all found myself among a tribe of savages, where I was present at a ferocious battle. However, I was not in the slightest danger, since I was both invisible and invulnerable. From time to time I looked at myself, that is to say, towards the place where my body would have been if I had had one, and I was able to assure myself that I no longer had one. I thought of visiting the moon, and immediately found myself there. I saw volcanic soil, extinct craters, and many other details, which were evidently the reproduction of things I had read or engravings I had seen. But they were all strangely enlarged and brought to life by my imagination. I was perfectly aware that I was dreaming, yet I was far from convinced that there was nothing veridical in what I saw. The admirable distinctness of everything I looked at made me wonder whether perhaps after all my soul really had temporarily quitted its terrestrial prison. If this were the case, it would after all be no more marvellous than many another mystery of creation. I thought of various opinions of the ancients on this subject, and remembered the following passage from Cicero:

Si quis in caelum ascendisset, ibique solem, et lunam, et sidera prope vidisset, hoc tamen sibi injucundum fore, ni aliquem qui narraret habuisset.

(If someone had ascended to the heavens, and had had a close view of the sun, the moon and the stars, this would nevertheless give him no pleasure if he had no one to whom he could recount it.)

I immediately wished to return to earth, and found myself back in my room. For a moment I had the strange impression of looking at my sleeping body, before taking possession of it again. Soon after that I dreamt that I had got up and, pen in hand, was writing a minute account of all that I had seen. Finally I really woke up. Almost immediately innumerable small details of my experience, which a moment before had been perfectly distinct, vanished from my memory. (pp. 369-370)

If it is correct to classify this experience as an out-of-the-body experience, it is nevertheless atypical in one respect: it is unusual for the subject to imply that his out-of-the-body experience, even if it occurred during sleep, was subsequently subject to the same sort of amnesia as a non-lucid dream. On the contrary, it is more usual for a subject to say that his out-of-the-body experience was more memorable even than everyday waking experience.

VIII

Subject E

In this chapter we shall consider the lucid dreams and out-of-the-body experiences of one of the Institute's own subjects. We shall call this subject 'Subject E', continuing the alphabetical series started by Celia Green in her book *Lucid Dreams*.

Subject E describes the origin of her lucid dreams as follows:

Since childhood I have occasionally had dreams accompanied by awareness that I was dreaming. In my mid-twenties, and probably as a result of two events which happened then, these 'lucid' dreams increased in frequency and significance, and other strange dream-like experiences started to occur. Subsequently I discovered that others have reported strikingly similar experiences known as 'out-of-the-body' experiences.

... As a child I would sometimes realise I was dreaming just prior to waking; so real did the dream-objects appear that it almost seemed possible to bring them back into the waking world by holding on to them. By the time I was in my teens awareness of dreaming was occurring in deeper states of sleep, sometimes in association with gliding or floating episodes.

Gradually, I took an increasing interest in my dreams, eventually coming to appreciate something of their psychological significance. The unconscious mind seems to respond to such interest: the dreams become richer in quality, it becomes easier to recall dreams on waking and, reciprocally, there begins to arise during dreams some recollection of waking life as a distinct experience.

Subject E offers the following comments on how to initiate lucid dreams, or at least to increase the probability of their occurrence:

Another factor favouring lucid dreaming is one's attitude to the question while awake. Thus if one concentrates on the idea that during dreams awareness of the fact will arise, resolving to respond to any incongruity by considering whether one may be dreaming—then this seems to penetrate into the unconscious mind with the desired effect. A similar thing is true of reflections as to why one failed on a particular occasion to become lucid—generally I find this is because I had failed to consider the question deeply enough (perhaps without realising it at the time). Then on subsequent occasions one tends to recall these reflections, leading to the deepening of awareness, both critical and intuitive, and the onset of lucidity. Furthermore, any intentions regarding experiments are best formed in advance; this also saves time wondering what to attempt when the occasion arises.

It is interesting to compare Subject E's attitude towards other people in her lucid dreams with that of Hervey de Saint-Denys. As we mentioned in the last chapter, the Marquis had some difficulty in realizing that the people in his dreams had no independent existence. Initially Subject E had what seems to be the more common attitude that other people were only figments of the imagination, to be treated accordingly.

In my early lucid dreams I tended to feel contempt for the dream-people: 'I am dreaming, and you are not real!' I would inform them.

Later her attitude changed somewhat as she came to regard the personages in her lucid dreams as being potential sources of information from her own subconscious. The following is her account of the lucid dream which marked the turning point in her change of attitude:

A later lucid dream ... concerned an Indian girl. Curious as to how she would respond to questioning, I asked: 'Who is your favourite composer?'—and was quite taken aback on her replying 'Schubert', instead of the answer I would have given. Yet her answer foreshadowed a deepening love of some of Schubert's music. Thus I came to feel that one could hold psychologically meaningful converse with lucid dream people, to regard them as symbolising aspects of my unconscious or subliminal mind.

The following is a more recent lucid dream illustrating Subject E's later attitude to the people in her lucid dreams.

While walking with two companions, a woman and a young man, I realised I was dreaming, and I decided to find out what they thought about the situation—did they realise this was just a dream? To my surprise they replied unhesitatingly that they did. I addressed the young man: 'But you only realise this through me.' 'No,' he replied, 'on the contrary, you realise it through me!—for example, there's a river round the corner which is not so in reality, but I have taken this from 1952/3.' (I did in fact live near a river at that time.)

--✦--

The lucid dreams of Subject E, like those of other habitual lucid dreamers, are generally characterized by a high degree of perceptual realism.

Subject E makes the following general comments on the perceptual texture of her lucid dreams:

The imagery of my lucid dreams is as a rule highly realistic, and—as indeed is the case with all my dreams—always in colour. There is nothing vague or indefinite, and wherever one looks one sees vivid, yet natural, detail and colour, even under the closest scrutiny. A frequent type of lucid dream is of walking or floating through beautiful scenery; this is comparable with the waking experience of visiting some unfamiliar, lovely, place. Here is a typical example . . . :

'While walking along a lovely tree-lined avenue I realised I was dreaming, and a sense of peace filled me. It was an autumn scene, and the ground was carpeted with crisp, brown and golden leaves. Eventually the avenue opened into a brilliant sunlit glade; a sparrow alighted on my hand and I observed closely its natural appearance and the subtle colouring of the feathers. Surveying the scene I felt a sense of wonder that it was possible to behold—purely in imagination—such vivid detail and beauty.'

Nor have I ceased to feel this sense of wonder at such times.

As well as the visual sense, the auditory and tactile senses seem fully operative; gustatory, olfactory and thermal sensations also occur but less intensely; whilst there seems to be an immunity from pain (beyond a slight degree), which is rather curious since practically every other aspect of waking experience is so well imitated. . . . I have observed in a general way that, for example, one isn't hurt by jumping or falling from a height, and that hitting or pinching oneself produced little sensation.

The following is a lucid dream in which Subject E deliberately sought to experience pain, thermal, gustatory and olfactory sensations:

Strolling along in some seaside resort I realised it was a dream. The sea looked dull, which struck me as most unusual for a lucid dream, although I noticed a glow developing to the east. I gazed down at the beach far below, and considered jumping, but demurred at the thought of the unpleasant falling sensation, which would doubtless be real enough although I knew I could not hurt myself. I walked on until I came to a path, which I descended. Noisy band music was playing, and I became aware of a cool breeze—a definite thermal sensation I reflected, and decided to investigate other effects. On reaching the lower promenade I tried hitting my leg with a stick; the sensation felt fairly realistic on the first stroke, but diminished to nil thereafter. I paddled in the sea, noting the coolness of the waves. My next aim was a gustatory sensation. Espying a jar of smallish (raw) plums on a counter I took one and began eating. The yellow flesh had a distinct plum flavour, although not quite as intense as one would expect in waking experience. While still eating (the plum increasing in size) I awoke, precluding any seeking of olfactory sensations.

Subject E remarks: 'Gustatory sensations occur quite frequently in my non-lucid dreams. I often remember dreaming of eating and drinking, seemingly with quite the intensity of waking life ... In lucid dreams however, one does not feel inclined to waste time eating and drinking, although this seems quite realistic when the occasion arises.'

It is interesting to note that Subject E, like Hervey de Saint-Denys, remarks on an almost complete absence of pain sensations in her lucid dreams.

The following is a lucid dream in which Subject E deliberately tried to produce pain sensations in a lucid dream:

I dreamt I was in the kitchen of a house where I used to live ten years ago. I became lucid, and in spite of my decision otherwise, felt a strong inclination to try to settle the question of pain in lucid dreams. I couldn't spot a pointed knife so picked up a metal skewer, and, trusting more or less to the immunity principle, tried to drive it into my hand—but somehow it would not pierce the flesh. To avoid any possible distraction from the other, mildly curious, people present, I went outside. Placing my left hand palm down upon the ground ... I raised the skewer high and plunged it down with all my force, over and over again; but the desired effect eluded me, and I felt only an occasional slight pressure. I decided on new tactics: plunging the skewer into the ground a few times in succes-

sion, observing the holes made, then at the next
strike quickly slipping my hand underneath—yet
still, incredibly, the skewer would not pierce the
flesh, tending to slide down between my fingers,
or off the edge of my hand, or getting obstructed
by a bone. This procedure I repeated many times
—then, at last, success! My hand was pinned
to the ground, the skewer having entered about
the middle of the hand between two bones—and
all I felt was the vaguely unpleasant sensation of
the skewer sliding through, and of having my
hand thus transfixed. I then drew out the
skewer, and examined the gory hole—it was indeed right through my hand (about ¼″ diame-
ter)—not actually bleeding, just some half-con-
gealed blood. The idea crossed my mind: no
pain and little bleeding, as is alleged can happen
under hypnosis. Mission completed, so to speak,
I awoke.

It is not impossible for Subject E to experience realistic pain sensations in a lucid dream,
however, as the following example from an earlier dream illustrates:

I realised I was dreaming, and recalled my intention (formed a few days previously) to investigate the possibility of inflicting pain on myself
in a lucid dream, preferably by knife. Finding
myself outside a kitchen (unfamiliar to me), I
entered and selected a knife—then hesitated.
For, although knowing I could not harm myself,
and accustomed to immunity from pain in lucid
dreams—nevertheless, deliberately to court the

sensation of pain in this way seemed quite another matter and, I imagined, might well induce considerable pain. Gingerly I tried the point of the knife against my arm, producing a disconcertingly real sensation. I therefore experienced great reluctance to carry out my intention, heightened emotionally by the memory of a distressing news item (concerning stabbing) of the day before....

Notwithstanding the high level of perceptual realism in Subject E's lucid dreams, she notes that departures from total realism do sometimes occur. She makes the following general remarks on this topic:

Despite the high degree of realism, fantastic elements do sometimes occur: e.g. the contraction of a path along which one is walking, the stepping directly into scenery depicted on a television screen. These effects are usually meaningful I find and, indeed, more interesting than a too rigid realism. Further, some parts of the surroundings not engaging the attention may later be found to have varied, rather in the manner of ordinary (non-lucid) dreams.

Subject E makes the following comparison between the degree of perceptual realism of her lucid dreams and that of her non-lucid ones:

I would say, also, that many of my ordinary dreams are just as vivid, realistic and coherent as my lucid dreams (and possibly more dramatic), but the awareness that one is dreaming (apart from tending to change the nature of the events) undoubtedly has an enhancing effect, perhaps deriving from the heightened observation.

Like a number of other lucid dreamers Subject E notes that there may be a certain difficulty in reading in lucid dreams. She also makes the interesting point that 'reading in lucid dreams, and remembering the words, seems more difficult than in ordinary dreams—perhaps this is because one tends to look in these circumstances for something specially significant'. It may also be, of course, that the lucid dreamer, having a critical awareness which the non-lucid dreamer lacks, is more demanding in what he will accept as meaningful written material, and the subconscious therefore has to make a correspondingly greater effort in order to present acceptable written material. Also, the subject's memory of lucid dreams on waking, unlike that of non-lucid dreams, is usually said to be comparable to his memory of waking life, and this again might mean that the subconscious had to 'try harder' in order to produce written material that would stand up to retrospective scrutiny on the part of the waking subject.

Subject E characterizes the emotional range of her lucid dreams as follows:

Realisation that one is dreaming brings a wonderful sense of freedom—freedom to try anything in the extended range of experience available without fear of any harm, except possibly fear of the *sensation* of pain until discovering as I did an almost complete immunity from pain. Floating or flying of some kind seems to be the most natural and delightful activity; I also used to like diving into the sea from a great height. Later I came to recognise in lucid dreams a splendid opportunity for trying experiments in various forms of control over the dream-objects (including the dream-body). The nature of lucid dream experience may range up to the mystical, whilst there seems an inherent resistance to anything erotic.

Subject E considers that her intellectual state, by which I mean the degree to which the normal contents of her waking mind are accessible to her, varies between one lucid dream and another, and even within the same dream. She says that even in her 'worst' lucid dreams, 'I find my clarity of mind sufficient to realise that the dream-objects and events are wholly imaginary, to think logically and do calculations correctly, to remember my name and general details of waking life.' In her better class of lucid dreams 'the range of analytical thought increases, and more specific details (including the date) become accessible to the memory'.

Like other lucid dreamers, she seems to find a particular difficulty in remembering very immediate details of her waking life, and remarks that it is only in her very best lucid dreams that she can 'trace through the events of, say, the preceding day (unless they were unusual or specially interesting) and it may take a great effort of concentration to do this correctly.'

※—❦—※

Subject E has a considerable degree of control over her lucid dreams.

She has evolved a technique very similar to that of Hervey de Saint-Denys for altering the dream scenery at will. She writes: 'It is ... possible to achieve a different environment by closing one's eyes and concentrating imaginatively.'

Subject E also uses the technique of covering her eyes in order to wake out of a lucid dream. The following is her description of this technique and its results:

The method, which I discovered quite by chance in an ordinary dream while hiding from pursuers, consists in covering my eyes with my hands and withdrawing my thoughts from the dream. There would follow a prolonged and most unpleasant sensation as though trying to get back into my body which I could sense but not move. Thereafter in unpleasant dreams I tended to remember this method for escape, and I also experimented with it in lucid dreams. With repetition the transition became quite easy, although sometimes instead of waking up I would find myself in a different dream, not necessarily lucid.

Like Oliver Fox and Subject B, whose experiences were discussed by Celia Green in her book *Lucid Dreams*,[1] Subject E has developed a kind of control of her lucid dreams which consists of producing what would be called psychokinetic phenomena if they occurred in waking life. She describes her development of this form of control as follows:

Having noticed how in ordinary dreams the objects sometimes seemed to respond to my thought, it occurred to me to attempt this deliberately in lucid dreams, trying to influence objects to move from place to place or to transform themselves. I discovered that a certain attitude . . . seemed necessary, otherwise the desired effect tended not to occur, or not correctly, or there might be a delayed action.

Subject E characterizes the requisite state of mind for inducing these 'psychokinetic' effects

[1] Op. cit., pp. 104-7.

in lucid dreams as follows: 'A certain balance of attitude seems necessary—expectancy without anxiety, intense concentration of imagination but no effort of will.'

She later adopted the same attitude, both to help induce out-of-the-body experiences, and to try and elicit ESP impressions when in the ecsomatic state.

To return to her account of the development of 'PK' effects in lucid dreams:

One dream I remember particularly in this connection featured a 'Wise Old Man' figure and a bird, which I commanded to come, but it would not—not until I adopted a more invocatory attitude. One's degree of control seems to improve with practice, both on the whole and within a particular dream. Thus on trying to induce an object to rise from the table and come into one's hand its flight may at the first attempts be rather uncontrolled. Objects can also be induced to vanish or appear, pens to write without support, birds to alight on one's hand and perhaps to speak, and so on. The dream-body may be levitated in various ways: e.g. on one occasion I succeeded in walking up a wall, across the ceiling and down the opposite wall.

The following is Subject E's account of a lucid dream in which she attempted to pass through the wall of a building:

I was out walking in some unfamiliar country place, when I realised it was a dream. For a while I scrutinised my surroundings, and then enjoyed a flying and floating session trying it with and without swimming motions of the arms. I passed a board with a place-name and other wording on it. Presently I remembered that I wished to try passing through a wall in a lucid dream, and looked about for a suitable wall. A short distance away stood a little building like a brick phone box, so I let myself float into it. At first there was no resistance then, to my surprise, I found I couldn't get right through; I felt as though groping in a black bog, and eventually I gave up the attempt. Presently vision returned, and I found that I was lying on the ground inside the little building; through the window I saw again the vivid blue sky and the board with still the same wording on it. I then let myself rise with the idea of passing through the roof— but the same thing happened again, except that this time I awoke.

～☙～

In the following lucid dream, dated Monday, January 9th, 1967, Subject E attempts to obtain evidence of ESP.

I dreamed of calling at my father's house. His startled expression and words 'I am not well' shocked me into awareness.—I felt rather as I do in the 'out-of-the-body' state, but considered that it might be merely a dream of being in that state. It seemed to be the Wednesday before my next visit. The clock showed 6.55 or 10.35 (approx.), neither of which was right, I decided. I asked my father to show me something (as evidence of ESP to be checked subsequently). He took me into the garden and dug a small hole, placing three bags therein. I observed the surroundings and a clocktower showing 7.50. Returning to the house, I picked up the cat. The postman delivered five letters, one containing a cheque for my father—and the question arose of the best way to cash it and of my doing so. I then awoke.

During my visit to my father on 14th January, he asked me if I would cash a cheque for him (something he has never asked me to do before). Moreover, it was for a special sickness benefit starting the previous Wednesday. (I had known nothing of this, nor had I told my father the contents of the dream). The rest of the dream appears to have no significance.

~☙~

In addition to her lucid dreams Subject E has had numerous out-of-the-body experiences.

Her first experience of this type arose out of what Celia Green has termed Type 2 false awakenings.[1] Here is a general account of her experiences of this type:

This consists of waking up, apparently in the usual way, then realising that something is

---

[1] Celia Green, *Lucid Dreams*, op. cit. pp. 121-4.

'wrong'; the atmosphere grows tense and eerie and hallucinatory effects appear. The first few times this happened I was very bewildered for, in spite of the odd effects, it was unlike a dream and, moreover, I seemed to be exactly where I would expect to be at that time of night. The thought that I must be awake and 'seeing things' made me panic and struggle to get free. When, exhausted, I just lay still for a while, everything would suddenly 'click' back to normal. Even in retrospect I was uncertain whether I had been awake or dreaming. Gradually I lost my fear of these experiences, realising that I need only relax in order to awake. I started trying little experiments, such as moving an object during the false awakening and checking its position subsequently, and concluded that my apparent movements and speech did not actually occur, and that the experience was a type of dream. The sense of transition when the dream-body and physical body were not in exact coincidence confirmed this. A similar phenomenon had also occurred in the drowsy state before going to sleep. The darkness which meets my gaze in the false awakening has sometimes been a heavy, unnatural one; usually there is some illumination (on one occasion I realised this was streaming from my eyes)....

The following is a particular example of a Type 2 false awakening experienced by Subject E:

I awoke to the realisation that the bedside radio was still on. Someone passed the door on the way downstairs. I turned the music low: strange, I thought, the radio being on this time of night—what *was* the time? I reached out of bed to look at the clock (about six feet away) but as I did so an eerie feeling came over me, and I hesitated; yet everything looked perfectly natural so I went ahead, against a mounting tension of the atmosphere, and picked up the clock—whereupon it suddenly changed in my hands! Hastily I put it down; its black dial had turned white and the hands moved to the 9 and 10. I recognised this was the false awakening. Pausing a moment to ponder the significance of the position of the hands (for I knew this could not represent the actual time) I dived back under the blankets. Monsters were pressing in on me, I called for help but could not wake up—not until I had seized hold of the monsters and fought them, and flung them on the floor.

Not that [Type 2] false awakenings are usually as nightmarish as this; at the other end of the scale, they may be so natural and lacking in eeriness as to completely deceive one. On three occasions (once as a child) I have experienced an hallucination after waking in the night, and it occurs to me this effect may be akin to the [Type 2] false awakening—perhaps a partial form of it.

Subject E's description of her Type 2 false awakenings is remarkably similar to those of other subjects who have reported this phenomenon. In particular I would draw attention to the following features of her description which are reported by one or more other subjects:

(1) a feeling of apprehension or tension in the atmosphere,

(2) a liability to see 'hallucinatory' effects,

(3) a characterization of the darkness of the room as 'heavy' and 'unnatural'. (Another subject has described it as being like 'black velvet—the air seems to have in fact substance as if you could take hold of it'.)

Oliver Fox believed that if one deliberately leaves one's bed during a Type 2 false awakening the experience turns into an out-of-the-body experience. Subject E also uses this technique for initiating ecsomatic experiences, and in fact regards Type 2 false awakenings as being identical with the ecsomatic state, except in so far as the subject's point of view is still located in the same position as that of the physical body.

The following is Subject E's account of the first two occasions on which her Type 2 false awakenings may be said to have turned into fully-fledged ecsomatic experiences. She had decided to make use of her false awakenings to try to make telepathic contact with X (a minister of her acquaintance):

I awoke in the night feeling rather elated about a talk on telepathy which I had heard the previous evening, when a curious thing happened—my hand sank through the bed and touched the floor. Standing up, I was intrigued to see a white horse at the foot of the bed. I felt as though in the false awakening, but without the feeling of tension. This horse could, I 'knew', take me to X, but I tried to direct it which was a mistake, for the experience degenerated into a lucid dream and then an ordinary dream, without finding X at all. In the morning I thought to the effect: I could have sworn my hand sank through the bed while I was still awake, yet I must have been mistaken. But I resolved to observe closely on any subsequent occasion.

As I lay awake one morning during the Christmas holiday I let myself relax deeply, trying to imagine I was floating on the sea and concentrating my thought on the experiment I wished to try. Gradually a numbness overcame me until I felt as though floating. My breathing and heartbeat quickened, then suddenly, my legs started moving (or so it seemed) down through the bed and back again, swinging through an ever-increasing angle. Excitedly I realised that what I had suspected before was indeed happening now, and I tried to stand up—with the effect of nearly terminating the experience. Quickly letting myself go the swinging process resumed, until at last my feet touched the floor and I stood free. (What a strange and wonderful feeling, like a butterfly newly emerged from its chrysalis.) At first I just stood by the bed, a little unsteadily, striving to see. Presently I could see the room clearly (it was not identical with the actual room); then I started swimming round and round close to the ceiling, gaining strength as it were. Now I was ready to seek X. I concentrated my thought towards him, but remembered this time to remain completely passive. I felt myself drawn swiftly along, until eventually I stood outside an unlikely-looking, pink and brown, scratch-marked door, with another door set at right angles on my left. Anyway, I entered the room—X was there!, over to the right, lying in bed; he smiled. I wondered if he could see an apparition of me, but reflected that he would probably be interested, rather than disturbed, at such an occurrence. I approached, touching him on the shoulder and calling his name. He looked suddenly startled and turned his head away, with a murmured 'hello' to me. The room was quite dim but a radiance shone round his head. I then said (as planned beforehand) and with some effort: 'I am experimenting, I am trying to reach you.' He replied: 'You shouldn't have done that'. Stunned by this cold response, I could think of nothing more to say, lost hold on the scene, and was awake. The time was 7.45 a.m.

Throughout the latter vivid experience I was intensely *aware*, with a delighted sense of freedom and power, and significance, such as I had never known in any lucid dream. Nor was there any break in awareness, either in the gradual onset or the sudden termination. Unfortunately I was not able to ascertain whether X had received any impression, for we never talked together again. in any case, awareness of telepathic contact (if such occurred) may not necessarily have arisen into his conscious mind.

There are a number of points of interest arising out of Subject E's account of her first out-of-the-body experiences.

Both an 'experimental' and an 'involuntary' ecsomatic subject have reported rather similar sensations of falling through the bed at the start of the ecsomatic state. The experimental subject is Subject A, who reports seeming to fall through the bed at the start of a deliberate attempt to 'visit' his son in another country.[1] A case of an involuntary subject who on two occasions had the experience of 'sinking at great speed through the bed, floorwards', at the start of his ecsomatic experiences will be found on page 37 of Celia Green's book *Out-of-the-Body Experiences*.[2]

Subject E's first experience also illustrates the fact that voluntarily induced ecsomatic experiences seem more likely to include non-realistic or 'fantasy' elements (in this case, the white horse) than involuntary or spontaneous ones.

Subject E's characterization of her intellectual state in the second experience as being 'intensely *aware*' is also reminiscent of many of the accounts of more involuntary experiences discussed in Celia Green's book.

~⊛~

---

[1] Cf. Celia Green, *Lucid Dreams*, op. cit., p. 170.
[2] Hamish Hamilton, 1968.

Subject E found that sometimes during a Type 2 false awakening she would apparently be able to 'read' the correct time off her clock-face, although the large and small hands of the clock tended to be interchanged. Here is her account of one such experience:

On one occasion ... I decided to have a look at the clock. But a cloth hid its face, so I said 'don't be silly!' whereupon the cloth disappeared—the hands read 8.22. 'This cannot be right' I reflected, 'for it is dark, and 8.22, morning or evening, would be light. . . .oh, I know!—perhaps the hands are reversed, the same as last time.' A few moments later I 'clicked' awake and sat up to look at the time—it was 4.41, an almost exact reversal of 8.22.

Subject E also reports one case of apparent precognition occurring in the ecsomatic state. The following is her account of this experience:

Finding myself one night in the [ecsomatic] state, I desired to see a suitable bungalow where we might live (we were anxious to move house at the time). After a travelling sensation I found myself hovering above an old terrace house in a London street. This is nonsense, I thought, for we would never consider moving *there*, and I tried to induce the vision to change, but to no avail. Then I 'clicked' awake.

Thus it looked as though my suspicion that

these strange experiences possessed an extrasensory element was unfounded. Several months later, however, something happened 'out of the blue' and we moved to just such a house as I had seen in the vision.

IX

---◆◆---

Some Cases of Ecsomatic Experiences

Since the publication of Celia Green's book, *Out-of-the-Body Experiences*, the Institute has received some fifty further cases of ecsomatic experiences. In this chapter we shall discuss these cases, and compare them with the four hundred or so analysed in the earlier book.

In general, the fifty new cases closely resemble the earlier ones. That is to say, they tend to exhibit the same psychological features.

The subjects tend to specify their position in the ecsomatic state with some exactness:

It is as if one had left one's body and was observing the whole incident as an independent observer somewhere outside and slightly above and in front of one's actual body.

... a little above it [my body] and a little to the right.

I was always in the same position—about a yard behind myself & about 2 yards up—looking over my own shoulder.

As these three quotations illustrate, a common factor in the subjects' apparent positions tends to be that they were above their physical body, rather than below it or to one side. The following two cases further illustrate this point.

I have, twice, in two different motor car accidents, both times I was fully ten feet up in the air, and, the first time I was very angry that I should have to come back into my body.

... I went into my bathroom and dropped something on the floor, I bent to pick it up—and was above myself looking down on my bent-over body, slightly to one side ...

Subjects often specify that they appeared to be near the ceiling, as in the following cases:

... the Doctor and Sister came in to have another look at me. While they were standing either side of my bed talking, I suddenly drifted out of my body and floated up between them to somewhere about ceiling height, and stayed there listening to what they were saying! ...

During the few minutes that this took, I was floating gently above them, looking down on the tops of their heads, and my body lying very still and pale on the bed between them. I remember distinctly that the 'body' did not move at all. I also recall seeing my temperature chart from above, held by a Sick Berth Attendant at the foot of the bed.

Then I slowly sank back into my body and went to sleep.

I was lying in bed one summer night aimlessly gazing at the neighbouring roof tops and it was light enough to see the colours. Suddenly I became rigid and slowly moved up to and pressed against the ceiling from where I could see down into the garden. Then I slowly went back down again.

. . . I was lying flat on my bed when suddenly I felt myself ascending almost to the ceiling and I was looking down on myself . . .

. . . I seemed to hang from the ceiling & saw a nurse & doctor taking bandages from my head but there were no bandages on me hovering above.

In particular, subjects sometimes specify being near a corner of the ceiling:

. . . I had an odd feeling of being up in a corner of the room, looking down at myself lying helpless in a chair . . .

. . . I was asleep one afternoon (shift worker). . . . I seemed to *float* out of myself, moving sideways out of my body until I reached the nearest wall on my *left* side—then I rose upwards turned over

—looking down—seeing myself fast asleep—travelled the length of the small room to the top of the door (6 feet high) then I stayed there a bit not wishing to go any further.

As Celia Green remarked in *Out-of-the-Body Experiences*, when the subject does appear to see his physical body from a height greater than that of the ceiling he does not usually mention passing through the ceiling.

I was somewhere high up and looking down on my body on my bed, but the body was small, as it would have been as seen from that distance.

Although the majority of subjects report being above their body in the ecsomatic state, this is not an invariable feature. In one class of case the subject may suddenly find himself sitting or standing 'opposite' his physical body, i.e. on the opposite side of the room and on much the same level as his physical body. The following two cases are of this type:

... I was unwell and lay down on a couch in the living room. I suddenly found myself sitting in an armchair the other side of the room. I saw my husband tip toe over, and bend over my sleeping body, to see if I was asleep. He then went quietly out of the room, taking no notice of me in the armchair.

Later on, I told him what had happened, and he confirmed that was what he had done.

On January the first I came into the sitting-room and sat in an easy-chair in front of the fire, when suddenly my body seemed to be two; I felt I was standing by the window,—standing looking at myself in the chair. I repeatedly tried to stretch over and touch the hand resting on the chair arm, but it wouldn't move to touch my 'outside' hand. ...

I saw my physical hand, but the feeling was in my other hand, where I was standing by the window.

❧

Many subjects report 'finding themselves' in their new ecsomatic position without any process of transition. In particular, the subject may describe waking to find himself in the ecsomatic state.

... I was awakened early one morning, to find that I had left myself, & was floating somewhere near the ceiling.

... mother came into my room, calling me to breakfast. I was floating about the ceiling and saw myself lying in bed.

... I have woken up at night and seemingly been floating in a reclining rigid position. The half light from the window of what-ever room I have been sleeping in has been displaced, or rather I am in a different position to what I should be in relation to it. Then as I concentrate and orientate myself I feel myself swing around, line-up with my body, a[nd] gently drop into it.

The following is a case in which the subject appears only to become aware of the ecsomatic state just as it is ending:

... I was awakened in the early hours one morning by the feeling that my body was just fitting itself back into its shell which was lying in my bed; I can still remember distinctly feeling my heels fitting back into their places.

The subject may also report finding himself in the ecsomatic state at night when he has not been asleep, but has merely been lying in bed, awake.

I was in bed, awake, at night, and suddenly was looking down on myself *on* the bed. I was curious about it, but so delightfully at ease and peace I did not question it. When I had to return I know I did not want to & tried to resist— which made return all the quicker.

... my wife & I had just got into bed when I suddenly found myself lying under the ceiling looking down at my wife reading ... the wife said afterwards she saw nothing unusual.

It was found in the earlier collection of cases that autoscopy, or the seeing of one's own body, was a prominent feature of many involuntary ecsomatic experiences. That is to say, the subject's physical body and its situation was very often the visual and emotional focus of interest during the ecsomatic state. This feature is also evident in the later collection of cases, as the following examples will illustrate:

... walking down the street of my home village I was suddenly aware of walking beside myself. This was so odd I remember looking into the face of my original self and realising it was me. Probably it lasted for about 3-4 mins and I was myself again ...

I felt my mental self or spirit soar over my body, separate & I looked down on it although my head was normally angled & I was looking ahead of me.

I looked down & saw the top of my brown felt hat & my hands loosely lying in my lap.

I could actually see myself sitting below on the back of the lorry ...

My body lay on the table and I could see them all operating. I was above them.

I left my body, or appeared to and looked down at myself kneeling there.

[I] distinctly remember seeming to hover over my own body while bearers put me on a stretcher while I watched from above.

I remember looking down and seeing myself in bed, with my mother sitting on one side and the doctor on the other—they were looking at me, not speaking, as though waiting for something.

As Celia Green remarked, if the subject does not find himself looking at his body at the start of his ecsomatic experience, he may deliberately 'turn round' in order to do so at some stage in the course of it. The following is a case from the present collection that may be of this type:

It started some time after I went to bed. I thought I woke up to find myself drifting towards the door. I remember looking at my bed and seeing my body still lying in it. I drifted out of the door and into another bedroom.

The following cases illustrate the subject's emotional relationship to his physical body during the ecsomatic state:

... I went to rest on my bed after a game of tennis, and almost immediately I found I was looking down upon my body some 2-3 ft below—I remember feeling quite 'detached' about the body on the bed which had no feeling at all—the real 'me' was the floating one above.

... I had the sensation that I—the essential part of me—was floating in the room. I could see my body lying on the bed & my mother sitting beside it weeping.

... my body was alive, yet I was definitely not in it, I felt sorry for the girl on the bed, it was as if I didn't want to go back, and yet I knew it was me.

It is usual for the subject to have a sense of well-being, and to feel relatively detached about the sufferings of his physical body, even when the ecsomatic state occurs during physical illness. For example one subject in the present collection, who had typhoid at the time of her experience, wrote that she 'felt light and perfectly well' in the ecsomatic state.

The following case, which occurred while the subject was anaesthetized and undergoing an operation, is unusual in the degree of emotional involvement she appears to have felt with the fate of her physical body.

... I seemed to stand at the head of my body, outside it, but not wholly detached, wringing my hands and weeping in anguished grief.

In some ecsomatic cases the subject appears to see things in the ecsomatic state that he would presumably not have been able to see in the normal way from his physical body. This may occur, for example, when the subject experiences the ecsomatic state while apparently unconscious. The following two cases, which both occurred while the subjects were under anaesthetic at the dentist's, illustrate this point:

After succumbing to the anaesthetic the next thing which I remember was seeing, from a distance of some ten feet, a patient in a dentist's chair with a dentist reaching over the patient and a nurse standing at the other side of the chair holding a large swab of cotton wool. I then remember awakening from the anaesthetic in the dentist's chair and a nurse handing me a swab of cotton wool.

... one day, at the dentist, when I was having a tooth out by gas, I had the feeling that I was a third party and was watching the operation from above. I even saw myself kick out at the dentist, almost kicking him in the shin, and when I asked him afterwards he said that this had, in fact, happened.

Sometimes the subject may deliberately seek information while in the ecsomatic state by 'travelling'. The following case illustrates how the subject may formulate such an intention while in the ecsomatic state:

I wondered where my brother was and decided to look for him and moved from above my bed through the door out on the landing and looked down the stairs ...

In one case in the present collection the subject experienced the ecsomatic state while in Exeter Cathedral, and appeared to rise to the level of 'a beam or piece of structure' up in the roof:

I smelt something dry & musty & saw, but I think not with eyes, dust in clumps, white and grey along this bar.

⤙⊛⤚

A number of subjects from the earlier collection reported inducing the ecsomatic state voluntarily or semi-voluntarily by means of relaxation procedures. One further such case appears in the present collection. The subject describes his relaxation procedure as follows: 'I lay down in bed and relaxed completely, starting on my toes and working up to my head.' After an initial success in which he appeared to rise a few inches above the bed, he did not achieve any further results of this kind for five months. Eventually, however, he had the following experience:

... I woke up again and found myself staring at something flat, white with thousands of little pin pricks or bristle marks in it. Well I was laying wondering what it was, because my eyes were just a few inches from it.

Well the thing I was staring at turned out to be the ceiling, so again I tried to control it, but everything went black and I fell asleep.

X

ESP and the Alpha-Rhythm

In my book *Science, Philosophy and ESP*[1] I made the prediction that the electroencephalogram (EEG) of the conscious ESP state would be found to be characterized by an accelerated alpha-rhythm.

Since this book was first published in 1967, this prediction has been confirmed by two experiments carried out in America by Rex Stanford and others.[2]

The subjects of both Stanford's experiments were students at the University of Virginia. In the first experiment thirty male students took

---

[1] Hamish Hamilton.

[2] Rex G. Stanford and Carole Ann Lovin, 'EEG Alpha Activity and ESP Performance', *Journal of the American Society for Psychical Research*, Volume 64, Number 4, October 1970, pp. 375-84, and Rex G. Stanford, 'EEG Alpha Activity and ESP Performance: a Replicative Study', *Journal of the American Society for Psychical Research*, Volume 65, Number 2, April 1971, pp. 144-54.

part, ranging in age from nineteen to thirty, and in the second experiment forty male students, mostly undergraduates.

Each subject was required to make a total of fifty guesses of standard Zener cards, each of which bears one of the five symbols: star, circle, cross, wavy lines and square.

Subjects made their guesses while lying down in a darkened room, and a recording was made of their EEG while they made their guesses. Each subject was required to relax for about four minutes in the darkened room before starting to make his guesses, and during this period his alpha-frequency was measured, to provide a 'base-line' or norm for that subject with which his alpha-frequency during the guessing period could be compared.

In both experiments it was found that the subjects who scored above chance on the card-guessing tended to show an acceleration in the frequency of their alpha-rhythm while they made their guesses compared with their normal base-line as measured before the start of the experiment. Furthermore, it was found that the better the subject's performance in the ESP test, the greater was the degree of acceleration shown by his alpha-rhythm. These results were significant at the 1 in 100 level in both experiments.

It is interesting to note that in Stanford's experiments, the subjects' overall alpha-frequency was not found to correlate with success or lack of it at the ESP task. In other words, it was not people with fast alpha-rhythms who were found to be better at ESP in this situation than people with slow ones. It was people whose alpha-frequency was *accelerated* above their own pre-test base-line who did better at the ESP task.

This result is also in line with the predictions made in *Science, Philosophy and ESP*. As I wrote at the time: 'The changes that we have predicted will occur in the conscious ESP state should be assessed by reference to the normal range of the individual, not by reference to some statistical norm of the whole population.'[1]

---

[1] Op. cit., pp. 154-5.

Index

About the Author

Born in 1942 at Stanton St. John, Oxford, Charles McCreery was educated at Eton College and New College, Oxford, where he read philosophy, psychology and physiology. Since 1964, he has been Research Officer at the Institute of Psychophysical Research, Oxford. He is the author of one other book, *Science, Philosophy and ESP*.

OUT-OF-THE-BODY EXPERIENCES

Celia Green

A fascinating, detailed study of psychical and psychological value, documenting cases of emotional and intellectual experiences that took place while the subject was out of his body.

"The present volume is the first in which contemporary instances are collected, collated and studied . . . the results are extraordinarily interesting, stimulating and well worth examining by the reader."

— *Times Literary Supplement*